The Unknown Prophet

To order additional copies of
The Unknown Prophet, Revised and Updated, call **1-800-765-6955.**

Visit us at **www.reviewandherald.com**
for more information on other Review and Herald® products.

The Unknown Prophet

Revised and Updated

Delbert W. Baker

REVIEW AND HERALD® PUBLISHING ASSOCIATION

Since 1861 | www.reviewandherald.com

Published by Review and Herald® Publishing Association, Hagerstown, MD 21741-1119

Review and Herald® titles may be purchased in bulk for educational, business, fund-raising, or sales promotional use. For information, e-mail SpecialMarkets@ reviewandherald.com.

The Review and Herald® Publishing Association publishes biblically based materials for spiritual, physical, and mental growth and Christian discipleship.

The author assumes full responsibility for the accuracy of all facts and quotations as cited in this book.

This book was
Edited by Dwain Esmond and Ray Woolsey
Copyedited by James Cavil
Cover Designed by Bryan Gray/Review and Herald® Design Center
Cover art by Thinkstock.com
Typeset: 11/12 Berkeley Old Style

PRINTED IN U.S.A.

17 16 15 14 13   5 4 3 2 1

Review and Herald Cataloging Service
Baker, Delbert W.
The unknown prophet: revised and updated

Foy, William Ellis, 1818-1893.   2. Millerite movement.
3. Blacks—Social conditions.   4. Blacks—Religion.   I. Title.
286.2'0924   [B]

ISBN 978-0-8280-2742-7

CONTENTS

Appendix

Prefaces

More than 25 years ago Delbert Baker's groundbreaking biography of William Foy was first published. It removed several mistaken perceptions about Foy, including that he, like Hazen Foss (the other man God called during the Millerite movement to be His prophetic witness) rejected God's call. Not so, as Baker's research conclusively demonstrated. On the contrary, Foy accepted God's call, shared what he had been shown, and remained a Freewill Baptist minister his entire life.

Readers also will discover the social challenges that Foy—a free-born Black living in pre-Civil War New England—faced in addition to the already-prevalent skepticism of Millerites toward anyone claiming to have visions. In addition, illuminating insights into the graphic prophetic visions God gave Foy, including comparisons to later visions received by Ellen White, await the reader of this book.

Several times I have stood by Foy's simple grave in East Sullivan, Maine. Not far from the cemetery where he is buried is the site of his last farm. Standing there, I have peered down into his well, the only tangible thing left on the property from Foy's time. The neatly built rock wall lining his well is an additional evidence of the careful type of person he was.

This revised edition of *The Unknown Prophet* is long overdue because through the retelling of the story of this humble man who was used by God, a new generation of readers will be challenged, inspired, and blessed by his life of committed service.

—James R. Nix, Director
Ellen G. White Estate

* * * * *

When I was a young man, I was taught that in the 1840s God offered the prophet mantle to three New Englanders. The first two of these, William Foy and Hazen Foss, I was told, declined the invitation and refused to serve the Lord in this special capacity. I know better now. In this volume Delbert Baker proves conclusively that although William Foy, the first man called, was reticent about public work, he did not say no to God.

From 1842 to 1844 he filled a special role, and then continued as a faithful Christian minister throughout his entire life.

Foy was an exceptional man, with powerful pulpit capabilities. He was also a truly converted, humble Christian. In the present work Baker paints the picture of a worthy disciple of Christ who, early in his ministry, was given several visions by the Lord. They dealt with heavenly themes, the glories of that better land, the judgment, the three angels' messages, and the need to be prepared for the early return of Christ. A little later Ellen Harmon (Mrs. E. G. White) was to experience visions on these same subjects.

This is a good book. I believe that as we become better acquainted with William Foy we will also become better acquainted with William Foy's God. And that, of course, is the purpose of this book. I heartily commend it to you.

—Robert W. Olson
Former Secretary, Ellen G. White Estate

* * * * *

Seldom does one encounter a book that so clearly taps the mainsprings of spiritual history as does this manuscript. *The Unknown Prophet* concerns not just a life but an experience of fundamental concern to the Seventh-day Adventist Church. The writer serves us nobly not only by his meticulous attention to data and detail but by his graphic portrayal of the socioreligious attitudes of Millerite times, his firm debunking of the many negative myths surrounding the ministry of William Foy, and his focus upon prophecy as a legitimate and highly functional element of remnant vitality.

One senses that in this book Delbert Baker has a dual mission, (1) that of vindicating the image of Foy, often thought of and referred to as a failed prophet—a Black who could have been what Ellen White later became—and (2) that of confirming Ellen White and the church she helped bring about as the special people of God.

Black Adventism, the SDA Church in general, and, in fact, any connoisseur of the dynamics of church history will benefit greatly from reading this well-researched biography.

—Calvin B. Rock
Vice President, General Conference
of Seventh-day Adventists

Welcome to the revised edition on the life and times of William Ellis Foy. The title has been changed slightly to give distinction from the first edition. This volume is called *The Unknown Prophet, Revised and Updated,* in contrast to the original, *The Unknown Prophet.* If you have an appreciation for history, rare documents, and classic site and period pictures, then this updated and revised edition will be an appreciated addition to your library.

The Revised Edition

Since the first edition appeared in 1987 it has become clear that William Foy's life and message have maintained relevance to readers. The volume has received widespread interest from the general public, support from the religious community—Adventists and non-Adventists—and endorsement from academia. Additional interest has also been sparked in the places Foy lived. For example, since *The Unknown Prophet* featured a photograph of Foy's gravestone in Birch Tree Cemetery, tourist and historical touring traffic has noticeably increased in the Sullivan and Ellsworth, Maine, areas.

In the early 1970s I began researching the life of William Foy as a result of hearing about him while a student at Oakwood College (now Oakwood University) and later during my seminary studies at Andrews University. Initially merely an academic subject, the study of Foy developed into an enthusiasm, then blossomed into a passion—a passion to learn everything possible about the man, his times, and the thoughts and motivations that drove him.

The years that followed were filled with research excursions to divers New England locales, from the hustle and bustle of Boston to the quaint and quiet of Chelsea, Maine. I indeed learned much about William Foy, and the appearance of *The Unknown Prophet* in 1987 yielded the fruits of my research. The volume sold well, and in fact, sold out.

After *The Unknown Prophet* went out of print, people routinely requested copies of the book, and there was an ongoing fascination in the

Foy story. In particular, on several occasions the Adventist Historical Society requested that the volume be reprinted on demand. Subsequently, a copy of *The Unknown Prophet* was scanned and made available free of charge online. Yet that wasn't sufficient. It seemed that nothing short of a revised edition would fill the need.

A number of factors led to the updating of *The Unknown Prophet* in 2013: the 150th anniversary of the Seventh-day Adventist Church; the discovery of a heretofore-unknown photograph of Orrin Foy, William Foy's son; several events commemorating the life and contributions of William Foy; and the encouragement of the Review and Herald Publishing Association in doing an updated edition.

Enriching Additions

In the revised and updated edition, while the essential text remains the same (with a few minor adjustments), the center picture section contains a special collection of rare photos and artwork that had been either unavailable or inaccessible in this convenient a manner at the time of the printing of the first edition. The reader will find the collection valuable for contextual understanding and orientation.

The appendix in this edition contains new and/or valuable documents requested repeatedly over the years. The Foy pamphlet *Christian Experience* has been available but little known by the public, and a poem by Foy entitled "Egypt's Land" was recently discovered. Crucial to an understanding of Foy's faithfulness to his prophetic calling is the 1906 D. E. Robinson interview with Ellen G. White.

Also included in the appendix are excerpts from the first history of Seventh-day Adventists by John Loughborough that provide an illuminating view of Foy by an early Adventist. An unpublished monograph written by a local historian in Maine provides insights on the Foys. The appendix is rounded off with a comprehensive Foy chronology, a bibliography, and a guide to online resources.

Timeless Appeal

The Foy story has all the drama and pathos of modern fiction—and it is true. It is situated in a turbulent epoch in American history when the nation was divided over the fundamental questions of slavery, equality, and human dignity. It portrays the saga of a reticent young man of color called to give a specific message at a specific time in history. It describes the travails of a young minister in the Advent movement during the middle 1800s who had the triple strike against him of having to proclaim an unpopular message, at an unpopular time, while being of an unpopular ethnicity. The story delves into the mind-set of the struggles and convolutions of a person who had to minister while battling on the controversial fronts of race and religion—an often fraught blend.

Beyond this, the Foy story features the fascinating encounter of one person who received special insights from heaven encountering another who received similar revelations. With wonder the reader experiences their chance but fortuitous meeting. From a historical perspective the Foy story takes one into the oft-meandering path of a character in history overlooked or misunderstood for decades—until finally resuscitated and given a fair hearing. The redemptive and cathartic power of this moment is moving.

Interest Points From the Foy Story

After the first edition of the Foy story was published, during numerous talks, seminars, workshops, and presentations about Foy's life and experience people reflected similar, almost universal reactions. The following general areas of interest help to provide the background for this revisiting of the Foy story.

Color and Calling: Inevitably people were intrigued by the idea that a person of color was the recipient of the gift of prophecy and the first to receive such revelations after the long period of silence since the New Testament era. It was an ideal platform to demonstrate the inclusive and diverse nature of divine encounters with the human family.

Truth in Time: Some listeners were inclined to believe that historical bias or prejudice was responsible for the fact that the Foy story was told fairly only in the 1980s, after so many years of silence. One doesn't have to be of the opinion that lack of knowledge or misinformation was owing to a cover-up or conspiracy, however. Rather it can be seen as being a confluence of historical occurrences that resulted in the belief that Foy died shortly after 1845. Simply put, Foy, after meeting Ellen White and recognizing that she had been given similar revelations but had even more insight and information, continued to speak and share his visions, but mostly retreated from the public's eye, commencing a quiet but effective ministry in the southern Maine region.

Researching the Story: History is an unfolding saga. It often takes its own time in the telling and revealing of its intricacies. Then for a story to be told, it takes someone to be interested, to research and work out the details, and finally to do the telling. Providence and events flowed together, and the story of Foy came out when it did and how it did. Everywhere I turned, when researching the story in the late 1970s and early 1980s, support and backing were readily provided—Oakwood University, Andrews University Archives, the General Conference Archives, the Ellen G. White Estate, Loma Linda University Archives, regional conferences, and the libraries and historical societies in Boston and Maine. The Review and Herald Publishing Association was particularly supportive, editing, cross-researching, and proofreading the manuscript and eventually publishing the first edition and now releasing this revised version.

When Ellen White Met William Foy: People were captivated by the thought of Ellen White as a teenager and her father, Robert Harmon, going to hear William Foy speak in Portland, Maine. Ellen White's reference to hearing Foy on several occasions and sitting by his wife, Ann, was a human-interest story that piqued the imagination. It humanized the story, rooted it in history, and showed the relation it had to the Advent movement that was so much a part of the social milieu of that time. It also revealed the Harmon family as progressive in their racial and religious thinking.

Interestingly, this encounter caused listeners to reflect on the positive impact that Foy's visions and recital would have had on Ellen White's also receiving and sharing them. Those meetings and the subsequent time, sometime later, that Foy spoke with Ellen White after hearing her relate what she had seen afford the reader the rare opportunity to see mutual prophetic affirmation in operation.

Foy and Race: Another point of intrigue was Foy's disclosure of people's perception toward him as a person of color and intimations of the opposition he encountered. Perhaps this is because people still and probably will always see race as an important factor in society. Further, being a Black Millerite, being a Millerite preacher, and preaching to mixed audiences of Whites and Blacks during pre-Emancipation Proclamation days when Blacks were routinely being lynched in the South and other places for associating with Whites has always been a central theme in the Foy forums.

Content of Foy's Visions: In my speaking engagements following the release of *The Unknown Prophet* the content of Foy's four visions always received a fair share of discussion. We have definitive information on the content of his first two visions and indirect information on his third, but only conjecture on his fourth. Nevertheless, people love to question and hypothesize as to what the visions meant, how and why they synchronized with Ellen White's formative visions, the content of the fourth vision, and why Foy received only four. I found the discussion of the visions and their content to be filled with theological and eschatological meaning and possibilities. What and whom Foy saw, his description of heaven, the judgment, and steps were meaningful to the Advent believers and, later, to Seventh-day Adventists. Then, of course, the whole conundrum of what the visions meant (or could have and should have meant) to Foy and early Advent believers is full of heuristic meaning.

Distinct and Different: People then, and even some now, have a tendency to confuse William Foy with Hazen Foss. Hazen Foss, the Caucasian Advent believer related to Ellen White through marriage, received visions after William Foy and refused to share what he had seen. After I researched the subject, it became very clear that Foy fulfilled his commission and that Foss, based on his own admission, did not, and gave up all interest in religion for the remaining years of his life. Both Foss's predecessor and successor had different experiences. Foy, who received revelations before Foss, had a specific and time-limited commission and met his divine commitment; Ellen White, who received divine revelations after Foss, had a far-reaching and lengthy commission and also fulfilled her divine commission. I found it one of the most enriching periods of my life to enter into their experience and to comprehend their story and work out its meaning for today.

Foy and Seventh-day Adventists: People often wanted to know if William Foy became a Seventh-day Adventist. There is no evidence that he did. Nor do we know what his understanding was of the Sabbath or about the additional light received by the movement that branched off from the Millerites and became the Seventh-day Adventist Church. There is simply no definitive evidence to answer those questions at this time. However, it is known that Foy was associated with the Freewill Baptists and pastored in various locales across southern Maine throughout the span of the second half of the nineteenth century. It is also confirmed that he remained a Christian until his death and was loved and respected in the area in which he ministered.

Visuals of William Foy: As of this date there is no known picture of William Foy. On the dust jacket of the hardcover of the first edition one can see the back of a man at a desk in a period study. That is not Foy, but simply an older pastor who modeled for the cover shot. In other volumes on Black Adventist history, there is a sketch of William Foy, but that is only a later artist's rendering of what he may have looked like.

Fortunately we now do have an image of what is believed to be William Foy's son Orrin, who is presumably in his 20s, likely around the same general age as Foy when he received his visions in 1842. It is probable that Orrin has some resemblance to his father. Perhaps someday a picture of William Foy will be discovered.

As mentioned earlier, there are two striking oil-on-canvas portraits of a Black Millerite husband-and-wife couple, William and Nancy Lawson, by artist William Matthew Prior (1806-1873), completed in East Boston, Massachusetts, in 1843. Nancy Lawson is held to be the cousin of William Foy. The citation by her picture reads "Nancy Lawson, nee Foy, born in Vassalboro, Maine, in 1810, was a first cousin to William Ellis Foy (1818-1893), who became a well-known Millerite preacher in Maine and Boston. She married William Lawson in 1827, and the couple had one child. The couple probably encountered Prior at a Millerite lecture or conference. . . . Although Boston was the epicenter of abolitionism in New England, racism still existed at all levels of society; the signature [of the artist, Prior] was both an artistic statement and an expression of the painter's moral values." Prior painted William Miller a couple of years prior to the Lawsons.

Foy for the Twenty-first Century

So the Foy saga continues. In this second decade of the new millennium the story is retold to old and new readers. It is the desire of the author that you might be inspired and challenged by the life of William Ellis Foy, because his story is the story of a man called to serve, to speak, to share. In spite of formidable obstacles and opposition he pressed on to do the task that God charged him with.

When I think of the William Foy's experience, the words of Teddy Roosevelt (1858-1919), one of Foy's well-known contemporaries who spoke of being determined in spite of obstacles, come to mind:

"It is not the critic who counts; not the man who points out how the strong man stumbles, or where the doer of deeds could have done them better. The credit belongs to the man who is actually in the arena, whose face is marred by dust and sweat and blood; who strives valiantly; who errs, who comes up short again and again, because there is no effort without error or shortcoming; but who does actually strive to do the deeds; who knows great enthusiasms, the great devotions; who spends himself in a worthy cause; who at the best knows in the end the triumph of high achievement, and who at the worst, if he fails, at least fails while daring greatly, so that his place shall never be with those cold and timid souls who neither know victory nor defeat."

William Ellis Foy, a life well lived—once unknown but now known. May his sincerity inspire you. May his vulnerability touch you. May his determination stabilize you. May his faithfulness motivate you.

Acknowledgments

The acknowledgments in the original volume remain the same, though several of the persons to whom I owe a debt of gratitude have been laid to rest. However, with this revised volume I want to thank: James Nix, director of the Ellen G. White Estate; his colleague, Tim Poirier, vice director and archivist of the Ellen G. White Estate; and Merlin Burt, director for the Center of Adventist Research at Andrews University. As in all my projects, my wife, Susan, is my constant inspiration and strong support. Also with this special edition my son, Benjamin Baker, Ph.D., assistant archivist at the General Conference of Seventh-day Adventists, has been an invaluable help. Further, the Web site that Benjamin established some years ago is a rich resource and is a repository of literally thousands of documents, photographs, citations, and references on Black Seventh-day Adventist history (see www.blacksdahistory.org).

May you be blessed as you read these pages.
—Delbert W. Baker
　Silver Spring, Maryland
　March 2013

Original Introduction

William Ellis Foy lived and ministered during the exciting and historic years of the mid-1800s. Monumental events took place during that period, which influenced the direction this nation was to follow for years afterward. This was also the time during which the foundation for the Seventh-day Adventist Church was laid.

God gave William Foy, a Black man in his early 20s, dramatic visions. These visions, received during the height of the Advent movement, preceded those given to Hazen Foss and Ellen White. They were lofty revelations, dominated by such themes as heaven, judgment, events before Christ's second coming, and God's watchcare over the Advent believers.

Little research, comparatively speaking, has been done on Foy's life. In church school curricula and denominational history books Foy's experience is often presented in a confused manner or omitted. Probably one of the reasons for this was that little was known about him. And what was known was often misinterpreted. At the beginning of my study of Foy's life (1978), there were no research or position papers available in Seventh-day Adventist libraries and archives. Fortunately, this situation has subsequently changed.

More than five years have gone into the preparation of this book. I have researched and analyzed all the known materials on Foy's life. My search has led me to archives, courthouses, libraries, and graveyards, to encounters with people in large cities and in obscure, out-of-the-way places. I visited places where Foy lived and worked throughout New England. My travels climaxed in Ellsworth, Maine, where Foy's tombstone is to this day.

His life story is inspirational and motivating. Throughout his experience Foy gives rich vignettes on how a Christian can face and profit from profound tests and trials. His life is a testimony to the reality of Jesus' power, even in the face of fear, intimidation, and insecurity. A minister of exceptional talent, Foy was willing to be used by God. His message transcends racial and theological camps.

Further, Foy's story provides a fresh look at Advent history from a unique perspective. It illustrates the broadness of God's plan for His children, and the marvelously rich multicultural approach He used during the beginning of Adventism.

A word about the format of this book. It is primarily biographical. It has been wisely said that a biography "fashions a man or woman out of seemingly intractable materials of archives, diaries, documents, dreams, a glimpse, a series of memories." I have tried to do this by telling Foy's story sequentially, while suggesting the important essence through his own words, historical conditions, revealing comparisons, character development, relevant quotations, and insightful details. A storytelling style was chosen over a heavily annotated academic style. For modern readers, necessary time has been given to set the historical and cultural context.

Further, a number of questions relevant to denominational history will be addressed, questions such as: What was the connection between the work of William Foy and Ellen White? What are some of the similarities between the messages of these two prophets? How might Advent history have been different if William Foy's message had been fully understood? What was the involvement of Blacks in the Millerite movement? What did William Foy's visions mean, and what message do they have for us today?

In the annals of history, notable figures are sometimes forgotten or overlooked. They are left as a legacy to be discovered in later years. Such is the case of William Ellis Foy. A Christian of great depth, a preacher of unusual ability, a spokesman for God with a special message, William Foy passed off the scene not as one who might have been used, but as one who was used: a mosaic in God's great design.

—Delbert W. Baker

THE

CHRISTIAN EXPERIENCE

OF

WILLIAM E. FOY

TOGETHER WITH THE

TWO VISIONS

HE RECEIVED IN THE MONTHS OF JAN. AND FEB. 1842.

PORTLAND:
PUBLISHED BY J. AND C. H. PEARSON.
1845.

Photoprint of the only known original of the pamphlet Foy wrote in 1845. It was published by the Pearson brothers, Advent believers who lived in Portland, Maine.

CONTEXT

"Again and again I have been shown that the past experiences of God's people are not to be counted as dead facts. We are not to treat the record of these experiences as we would treat last year's almanac. The record is to be kept in mind; for history will repeat itself. The darkness of the mysteries of the night is to be illuminated with the light of heaven."

E. G. White to A. G. Daniells
November 1, 1903

Line drawing of Boston skyline during Foy's time.

A Feel for the Times

Tuesday evening, January 18, 1842, William Ellis Foy, a young minister, met with a group of Advent believers on Southock Street in Boston, Massachusetts.

Twenty-three years of age and of an inquisitive mind, Foy enjoyed these gatherings and often contributed to them. They offered opportunity for prayer, praise, and Bible study. One of the most attractive aspects of these meetings was that while the audience was a mixture of Blacks and Whites, no one seemed to mind or notice color of skin. For William Ellis Foy this was particularly good—because he was Black.

While engaged in prayer during this meeting, Foy experienced his first vision. He was shown the glorious rewards of those believers who faithfully followed Christ. His visionary experience was witnessed by a local doctor, by Foy's wife, and by other believers who were present. The vision lasted two and a half hours.

Prior to the Great Disappointment, Foy received at least three other visions. Being young and Black, along with having a retiring personality, he began to feel the great weight of having to share with others what he had seen and heard. This experience proved to be the greatest challenge of his life.

Who was William Ellis Foy? Where did he come from? What was the nature of the society in which he lived? What was he shown in vision? What impact did his race have on his ministry? What task did God set forth for him? What was his relationship to Ellen G. White? And whatever became of him?

This is the untold story . . .

In a rural area near Augusta, Maine, in the year 1818, Joseph and Elizabeth Foy, aided by a local midwife, welcomed their first son, William Ellis.[1] There was nothing particularly auspicious about his birth—except to the parents. In those days a Black baby was nothing to get excited about. Times were difficult, money was short, and racial tensions were high. However, Joseph and Betsy Foy were free Blacks. And so their son was born free.

It is vital to our story to understand the social mind-set of the world into which William Foy was born. Some historical background will help us achieve a better understanding of his outlook and later actions. So let's take time to reconstruct the prevailing historical milieu.

Widespread and intensive change characterized the period of history in which William Foy was born. Nineteenth-century America—marked by reform movements, by territorial expansion, by racial conflict and division—was moving inexorably toward the Civil War. So diverse and infiltrating were the areas of change that no part of society remained unaffected. Socially and economically there was a flurry of activity. Of the 40-year period following 1820, it is said that America literally "burst at its seams." Populated areas just about doubled in size, with the total population increasing more than 300 percent. Eleven states joined the Union. A wave of migration spread westward and southward. Where before the general population lived in the countryside and worked the land, now people moved toward the cities to work in the factories that seemed to have mushroomed overnight. This along with a series of technological breakthroughs, revolutionized events to such an extent that people were left in a sort of social daze.[2]

Along with progress, these changes brought problems. A new sense of excited insecurity seemed to grip the country. Confronted with the need to adjust almost daily to these differing conditions, people began to sense a need for the lasting support that only religion could bring to their lives.

Another historical phenomenon during Foy's time were the religious movements! Religion in nineteenth-century America couldn't have been more varied. He witnessed a period of religious fragmentation unlike any in history. Of this time Richard Schwarz said, "The late eighteenth and early nineteenth centuries were rich in religious diversity. New sects proliferated. Rejecting established churches and dogma, proclaiming their return to Bible-oriented primitive Christianity, some of these groups developed into religious communes with beliefs and practices later shared by Seventh-day Adventists."[3]

America had long been a promised land for religious dissidents. From the Quakers to Jemima Wilkinson of the Universal Friends to Mother Ann Lee Stanley of the Shakers to Joseph Smith of the Latter-Day Saints to the spiritualistic, philosophical teachings of Emanual Swedenborg—the religious world ran a broad gamut.[4]

Mainline religious bodies, despite their religious plurality, were generally weaker in America than they were in Europe: "The Roman Catholics were in a minority, the Orthodox were very small, Lutherans were less prominent than in Europe, the Episcopalians were only socially important and far less represented than in England, Presbyterians were much weaker than in Scotland, and the Reformed represented but a faint reflection of their position in the Netherlands and Switzerland."[5] Significantly, the Methodists and Baptists were minorities in England yet comprised more than half of the Protestants in America.

A frontier revivalism followed in the wake of the Great Awakening in New England. Religious America was experiencing the same level of growth and unpredictable change as were other areas of social life.

Brimming with missionary zeal, religious America targeted three particular groups: first, the partially secularized descendants of immigrants who had come to the country in the Colonial period; second, Indians and Blacks, on whom religion was often used as a means to subjugate or control; and third, the new immigrants just arriving in America.[6]

Religious reforms tend to lead to social reforms. Charles Finney (1792-1875), one of America's most famous revivalists and the father of modern revivalism, preached not only salvation but reform. Reform cleansed society's sins as salvation cleansed people's sins. Temperance, education, the status of women, health, democracy, and communication were seen as areas in need of reform.

However, toward society's greatest sin the public developed an increasingly ambivalent attitude. This period focused on the slavery issue as never before. Even as the demand for slaves increased in the South, antislavery societies sprang up in the North. Slavery: bane or blessing? The answer depended on who you were and where you lived.

During these years, relations already tense compounded to such a pitch that they finally exploded in the Civil War. The institution of slavery, with its resultant discrimination and prejudice, elicited moves and countermoves from all quarters. Of this period it is said that "revolts, or conspiracies to revolt, persisted down to 1865. They began with the institution and did not end until slavery was abolished. It can, therefore, be said that they were a part of the institution, a kind of bitterness that the Whites had to take along with the sweetness of slavery. As the country was turning to Jeffersonian Republicanism at the beginning of the nineteenth century, many people believed that a new day had arrived for the common man. Some Negroes, however, felt that they would have to force their new day by breaking away from slavery."[7]

Unquestionably, these events affected Foy directly and indirectly. They had an effect on everyone, Black and White. History books are replete with the acts of violence and racial estrangement that took place during this period. It is sufficient to say that it was a dark period in our national life.

Long before Foy's time, Blacks such as Prince Hall, Benjamin Banneker, Absolom Jones, and Richard Allen issued strong denunciations against the slavery system. During Foy's early life, these tensions increased. Ministers, editors, and other leaders of public opinion, both Black and White, spoke out against the evils of slavery.

The abolitionist movement fought slavery persistently and effectively, vocally and in print. But there was also the less-visible resistance that slaves themselves gave: "Some slaves disguised themselves or armed themselves with free passes in their effort to escape. Others simply walked off, apparently hoping that fate would be kind and assist in their permanent escape. Some were inveterate runaways, such as the North Carolina woman who had fled from her master's plantation no less than 16 times. . . . While there is no way of even approximating the number of runaways, it is obvious that fleeing from the institution was one of the slaves' most effective means of resistance. It represented the continuous fight that slaves carried on against their masters."[8]

"The most sensational and desperate reaction of Negroes to their status as slaves was the conspiracy to revolt. To the Negroes who could summon the nerve to strike for their freedom in a group, it was what might be termed 'carrying the fight to the enemy' in the hope that it would end, once and for all, the degradation of human enslavement. To the Whites it was a mad, sinister act of desperate savages, in league with the devil, who could not appreciate the benign influences of the institution and who would dare shed the blood of their benefactors. Inherent in revolts was bloodshed on both sides. The Blacks accepted this as the price of liberty, while the Whites were panic-stricken at the very thought of it. Even rumors of insurrections struck terror in the hearts of the slaveholders and called forth the most vigorous efforts to guard against the dreaded eventuality."[9]

When Foy was 4 (1822), Denmark Vesey rebelled against slavery by leading a slave revolt in South Carolina, sending shock waves throughout the nation. When Foy was 10 (1828), William Lloyd Garrison, an abolitionist who later had a decisive effect on the antislavery movement, started his anti-slavery career. When Foy was 11 (1829), David Walker published his famous antislavery pamphlet *Appeal,* which blasted the slavery system and set national nerves on edge. When Foy was 13 (1831), Garrison published the first issue of his abolitionist newspaper, on New Year's Day in Boston. This paper, the *Liberator*, was destined to become second to none in agitating the slavery question. Every thinking person found the times most turbulent and vexing. To both enslaved or free Blacks, they were especially precarious.

These realities were factors that later caused William Foy much perplexity and anguish when he was confronted with God's special commission. Throughout his ministry he seemed constantly to be conscious of these tensions and pressure.

On the other hand, this was an ideal time for the development of religious truth. In 1831, William Miller began to preach a new message—the imminent coming of Christ. When Foy was 15 (1833), living in the Palermo, Maine, area, William Miller was given a license to preach as a Baptist minister. When Foy was 26 (1844), the Great Disappointment gave birth to a new Advent movement.

Foy's contemporaries also included the major Seventh-day Adventist pioneers: James White (1821-1881), Ellen White (1827-1915), Joseph Bates (1792-1872), Hiram Edson (1806-

1882), and John Andrews (1829-1883).

It is often difficult, because of one's very closeness, to understand the significance of the times in which one is living. No doubt this was true of William Foy. Little did he realize how momentous were the events he was witnessing, or the pivotal position he would occupy.

NOTES

[1] Vital records supplied by William Foy's death certificate, obtained from the state of Maine in November 1983.

[2] David Burner, *The American People* (St. James, N.Y.: Stoney Brook Press, 1980), Vol. I, chap. 11.

[3] Richard Schwarz, *Light Bearers to the Remnant* (Mountain View, Calif.: Pacific Press Pub. Assn., 1979), p. 14.

[4] *Ibid.,* p. 16.

[5] P. Damsteegt, *Foundations of the Seventh-day Adventist Message and Mission* (Grand Rapids: William B. Eerdmans Co., 1977), p. 4.

[6] *Ibid.,* p. 8.

[7] Burner, p. 163.

[8] John Hope Franklin, *From Slavery to Freedom* (New York: Alfred A. Knopf, Inc., 1980), p. 153.

[9] *Ibid.*

A typical rural scene from the New England countryside.

Family Ties

William Foy's birthplace in Kennebec County, near Augusta, Maine, was far removed from the oppressive conditions of the slave-holding states, as Maine had very few Blacks and virtually no slaves. Nor was Maine a state with a strong color consciousness. Because of the sparsity of Blacks living there, the White citizens seldom had to deal with the color question. That is not to say that in Maine there was no prejudice or racial problems, for there were. But while racism was existent, it was never as blatant as it was in the South, or even in the urban centers where Foy later lived.

The most significant fact relating to Foy's roots is that he was born a freeman in a free family. Although the boon of freedom was a prize that Blacks fought for, treasured, and defended, the free Black had his own unique burdens to bear. And these burdens greatly affected his worldview.

Foy's ancestral record is blurred and sketchy in parts—few records were kept of Black family lines. Yet for the times it is remarkably revealing. Because Foy became a recognized preacher, the census records provide a fairly clear document trail of him, his family, and their ages.

The Foys lived in a rural area to the north of Augusta, the capital of Maine. William Ellis appears to have been the eldest of three boys, with possibly one sister. According to the census, a number of other Foys lived in the same area—in-laws and other relatives—along with a small group of other Black families.[1]

The Foys owned a substantial plot of land and made their living from it. In those days it was common practice for entire families to live together and work the land communally. This was especially so for Blacks, as farming was one of the safest and most uncontroversial livelihoods available to them. Though by no measure were the Foys people of means, records indicate that there were numerous sales of parcels of land back and forth in the Foy family, usually for paltry amounts of money. This too was a common practice, for convenience in executing wills, disposing of property, and sharing of land with family or relatives. This simplified method of selling and buying property was quicker and more manageable than going to the courts.

While it is clear that the majority of William Foy's immediate and extended family were farmers, records indicate that some engaged in other occupations as well. Blacks living in the vicinity worked as victual servers, hairdressers, barbers, fishermen, and housekeepers. These were typical occupations for Blacks during this period. However, these urban jobs were supplemental to their work on the farm.

So William lived, learned, and grew up in a country setting—at least until the middle or late 1830s when, records indicate, he married and moved to Boston. But on the farm he no doubt developed the love for country living that remained with him throughout his life. Skills of farming and carpentry later proved to be an asset in providing a livelihood.

In his later years he gained a great deal of respect not only as a kind and thoughtful neighbor but also as a builder. Local records indicate that he built a house for one of the area families. And verbal tradition has it that he helped build the local rural church. He was also known to farm his land and share its products with the neighbors.[2]

Demographic studies reveal that at the beginning of the nineteenth century most Blacks lived in rural settings. It was only much later, with the increase of factory and city jobs complementary to the Industrial Revolution, that Blacks as well as Whites began to move in large numbers to the cities, especially to the cities and towns on the Eastern seaboard. Living in the country first then moving to the city Foy followed this trend.

That Blacks were still essentially rural during Foy's boyhood is demonstrated by the following statistics: in 1790 New York had 3,252 Blacks—2,184 were slaves, 1,078 were free; Philadelphia had 1,630 Blacks—210 were slaves, 1,420 were free. At the other extreme was Baltimore with 1,578 Blacks, of whom only 323 were free. Boston, the city where Foy later received visions, was unique; it was the only American city that could boast that it had no slaves at all. Of the 761 Blacks in Boston, all were free.[3]

Foy's ethnic background has a number of interesting aspects. In some accounts he is referred to as a "mulatto." However, the primary definition of mulatto is "the first generation offspring of a Negro and a white." According to the best original sources—census records, birth certificates, and family lines—Foy did not have parentage that would fit that description. Census records and his death certificate refer to him simply as being Black. His light complexion may have led some to refer to him as a mulatto.

All things considered, New England was a beneficial place for a young Black man in the 1800s. Slaves were known to have lived in the New England states from a very early date. Though the primary economic interest of these states was never in slavery as an institution, many entrepreneurs engaged in the general slave trade. Records have been discovered dating back as early as 1638, among which are particulars on a Salem slave ship's unloading several African slaves in freedom-loving Boston!

Blacks were also present before 1650 in Hartford, Connecticut, where they took part in the construction of houses and forts. By the latter half of the sixteenth century, the refugees who founded Rhode Island were using Blacks to help establish that colony. So some Blacks had been in the New England area for a long period of time, and some had known slavery.[4]

The records suggest that because of racial pressures or other motivating factors, the Foys migrated to the Augusta area, probably from the Boston area during the eighteenth century. At this time, Blacks with the name of Foy began to appear in the cities. Maine was an ideal place for a free Black family to settle, for land, privacy, and jobs were available there. In addition, slavery had virtually died out by that time.

During the 1800s Augusta was considered to be an important religious center. A variety of churches served the community: Baptist, Methodist, Congregationalist, Episcopal, Catholic, Freewill Baptist. Adjacent to the Foy property was an old church meeting house. Yet despite the fact that he grew up in a typical religious community, he wasn't converted until the age of 17, in 1835.

Just how religious were Foy's parents? His religious proclivity and free access to the local churches suggest that his parents were either themselves reasonably devout or at least accepting of their son's spiritual interests. After William's father died, his mother lived and traveled with him as he went from one pastorate to another.

When all available facts concerning William Foy are brought together—facts concerning the social and religious context of his day, his family history, and of his unbringing— a picture begins to emerge. It is a picture of a man who was being readied for a task—a task that was important and real and imminent!

NOTES

[1] *International Genealogical Index* (Maine, Massachusetts); U. S. census records of the 1800s for the state of Maine; 1850 index for Palermo, Maine.

[2] Lelia Johnson, *Sullivan and Sorrento Since 1760, p. 37.* The verbal tradition reference is a taped interview with local resident who recalled this tradition. However, it is factual that Foy owned land with a house on it.

[3] Franklin, *From Slavery to Freedom,* p.98.

[4] *Ibid.,* p. 63

CAUTION!!

COLORED PEOPLE

OF BOSTON, ONE & ALL,

You are hereby respectfully CAUTIONED and advised, to avoid conversing with the

Watchmen and Police Officers of Boston,

For since the recent ORDER OF THE MAYOR & ALDERMEN, they are empowered to act as

KIDNAPPERS

AND

Slave Catchers,

And they have already been actually employed in KIDNAPPING, CATCHING, AND KEEPING SLAVES. Therefore, if you value your LIBERTY, and the *Welfare of the Fugitives* among you, *Shun* them in every possible manner, as so many *HOUNDS* on the track of the most unfortunate of your race.

Keep a Sharp Look Out for KIDNAPPERS, and have TOP EYE open.

APRIL 24, 1851.

Placard issued by the Vigilance Committee of Boston showing the tenuous status of freedom.

Tale of a Freeman

I t became very crossing."[1] This was how Foy described the emotional dilemma that he faced when bidden to relate to others the visions he had received. The phrase "very crossing" carries the meaning of a decision that was extremely difficult, that was emotionally and mentally trying. It is difficult to really appreciate Foy's dilemma unless the circumstances causing it are examined.

Foy's position as a freeman was complicated by increasing tensions over slavery. The issue had grown so widespread, so pervasive, that virtually every area of life was affected by it. Years later Ellen White succinctly summed up the major social ill of this period in her watershed message on the race question, "Our Duty to the Colored People": "It has become fashionable to look down upon the poor, and upon the colored race in particular."[2]

It is sometimes believed that a free Black person in a Northern city during the 1800s would have had a relatively easy life. However, that was not the case. Life was difficult for free Blacks as well as for slaves—though in a different sense.

The term "quasi-free" can best describe the role of a free Northern Black. This term highlights their role confusion, their in-between state, a state that we might refer to as neither/nor. A free Black person was not a slave, but neither was he totally free, with privileges equal with Whites. He was somewhere in the undefined middle.

William Foy faced this societal and emotional dilemma in 1842. To accept the task of proclaiming visions to the world was a frightful task. Because, whether slave or free, Blacks placed themselves in a vulnerable and dangerous position when they undertook to communicate with, share ideas with, fellowship among, or lead Whites.

Statistics on free Blacks in the United States cast light on Foy's precarious situation. In 1790, the time of the first decennial census, there were approximately 59,000 free Blacks in the United States. About 27,000 were in Northern states, and 32,000 in the South. By 1800, free Blacks had increased approximately 82 percent, but following the year 1810 the rate of increase dropped sharply, a trend that continued through to 1860. Why? Essentially it was because of new and stringent laws against manumission (the release of a Black from slavery). Sadly, Whites had begun to view the increasing number of free Blacks with great alarm.[3]

The Northern cities of Boston, New York, Cincinnati, and Philadelphia were some of the key areas where Blacks concentrated. Many free Blacks were urban, doubtless because of the greater opportunities, both socially and economically, that were available in cities.[4] Young Foy himself was an example of that trend, for he moved to the Boston area and lived there for some three years (c. 1840-1842). Boston was one of the prominent centers for free Blacks and for reform and other social movements.

The status of a freeman was almost a contradiction of terms. His "freedom" depended precariously on the sufferance of Whites. Actually, by the time of the Civil War, the status of freemen had deteriorated to such a level that in some places differences in the de facto status of free Blacks and slaves were hardly discernible.[5] Several Southern states went so far as to require free Blacks to have White sponsors in order to reside permanently in the state. If a White person claimed, even fraudulently so, that a Black was a slave, there was little the freeman could do about it. A freeman lived with the fear of kidnaping, physical injury, or death, along with the fear of being reduced to servitude by the courts. Judicial ignorance or oversight could send a free Black back into slavery or worse.

Foy's movements, like that of all Blacks, would have been closely monitored. Control over free Blacks increased with each passing year. No Southern state allowed free movement. And in many Northern communities it was dangerous for freemen to travel lest someone think they were fugitive slaves. Many states went so far as to stipulate how long a freeman could be absent from the state. Any freeman who broke these restrictions faced stiff penalties.

A freeman was generally allowed the right to own and sell property. But in the judicial system the testimony of a freeman was not admissible in cases where Whites were parties. The disesteem in which freemen were held is illustrated by the fact that slaves, usually viewed as wholly irresponsible before the law, were allowed to testify against free Blacks. If there was one heartening aspect of the judicial system, it was that the higher courts, as compared to the lower, tended to be fairly lenient toward free Blacks.

Any local public act of insubordination on the part of slaves or free Blacks had a reverberating effect on the national racial scene. One historian had this to say of a notable instance: "If the rise of abolitionism had a positive influence on Negro evangelism, Nat Turner's slave insurrection in Virginia in 1831 had the opposite effect."[6] In short, if a slave was slapped in Georgia, freemen in Boston would feel the vibrations.

To enlarge upon this, Nat Turner's abortive revolt resulted in a mass of new legislation designed to secure the White community against any threats or dangers from free Blacks. "By

1835 the right of assembly had been taken away from almost all free Negroes in the South. They could not hold church services without the presence of a licensed and respectable White minister. Benevolent societies and similar organizations were not allowed to convene. In Maryland free Negroes could not have lyceums, lodges, fire companies, or literary, dramatic, social, moral, or charitable societies."[7]

Though these laws didn't have the same effect in Northern cities as they did in the South, any Black leader would have been aware of the stipulations and inherent dangers that accrued to him as a result of turmoil and suspicion generated in other places.

Other records reveal that "from 1830 to 1832 many state laws were enacted forbidding instruction of slaves, limiting Negro preachers, forbidding assembly of Negroes except when supervised by Whites, limiting slave hiring, forbidding drums, whistles, and musical instruments. These laws required prompt deportation of freed slaves and limited vocations and movements of freed Negroes."[8]

Free Blacks were limited in the ways they might make a living. There were restrictions on selling foodstuffs and certain other items. In some places there were restrictions against practicing certain trades or buying certain articles. Yet "despite these restrictions every state required free Negroes to work, and their means of support had to be visible."[9] Pennsylvania proved to be a bellwether state when in 1725 it enacted legislation requiring that "if any free Negro fit to work shall neglect so to do and loiter and misspend his or her time, . . . any two magistrates . . . are . . . impowered and required to bind out to service such Negro, from year to year, as to them may seem meet."[10] Other states went so far as to require free Negroes to post bonds as security against becoming public charges. Not only were adult free Negroes forcibly hired or bound out, but their children were taken and placed in the care of White persons.

The dilemma was a real one. It was aptly described in the following words: "In the two decades preceding the Civil War, White immigrants depressed wages and eliminated Negroes as serious competitors in several fields. The situation was alarming; some Negroes were actually starving; and behind the danger of starvation lay the danger of mob violence at the hand of desperately insecure immigrants."[11] Specifically, free Blacks seeking to satisfy the state's work requirements were nevertheless excluded from many trades by White-only unions. To obtain vital apprenticeships, training became extremely difficult. In fact, the president of a Cincinnati mechanic association was taken to court for the "crime" of helping a young Black learn a trade.[12]

The frustration Blacks experienced has been descriptively summed up by historian Lerone Bennett: "Neither fish nor fowl, neither slave nor free, Negroes in the North existed on a precarious ledge. At any moment they could be shelved off. Seldom in any country have men lived in such a vale of anxiety. Time and time again, Whites herded Negroes into groups and pointed to the city boundaries. Time and time again, immigrants, fresh from the boats, cracked the skulls of Negroes and burned their homes and churches. Some men said openly that the only solution to the 'Negro problem' was the 'Indian solution.'"[13]

In the midst of this gloomy picture stands out one great advantage for free Blacks in Northern communities. That was the opportunity, especially in Boston, to secure an education. As far back as 1787, Prince Hall and other Boston Blacks petitioned the Massachusetts legislature for equal school facilities. Early in the 1800s Whites in Boston taught Black children, both privately and in public institutions. In 1798 a separate school for Black children was established by a White teacher in the home of Primus Hall, a prominent Black. In 1800 Blacks established their own school, employing two Harvard men as instructors. The school flourished for many years.

Eventually, in 1820, the city of Boston opened the first public elementary school for Blacks. Antislavery sentiments soon attacked the practice of separate schools; and as a result, by 1855 both Boston and New Bedford permitted Black children to attend White public schools. However, the legislation stated that any district not so inclined could, by local option, establish segregated schools.

Probably one of the most mentally excruciating and socially embarrassing aspects of daily life that free Blacks had to deal with was the overall discrimination—being treated as if they were nonpersons—that they were forced to endure. With the obvious badge of color as an immediate identification point, Blacks were easily spotted and derogatorily pointed out.

Finally, there was the ever-present threat of real physical violence perpetrated on Blacks who "got out of line." The documented cases are too numerous and horrible to tell. The fear of violence was very real.

John Hope Franklin succinctly sums up the social gloom: "Thus Negroes went through the terrible ordeal of moving toward freedom. It cannot be said even of the most fortunate that they were entirely free. They suffered indignities and insults, legal disabilities and economic privations, violent physical and verbal calumniations. Their reactions, even when sober and considered, were the reactions of a frustrated, stricken people. The mistreatment of free Negroes was not sectional. At best the situation in the North was tolerable, but only in a relative sense: it was better than in the South. Small wonder there was so much despair."[14]

This then was the world that Foy grew up in, the conditions he was daily exposed to. With this picture we can better understand and appreciate the divine and human dynamics at play when God revealed to Foy visions that he was to share with the world. William Foy compacted a nightmare of reality into two sentences when he said: "Knowing the prejudice among the people against those of my color, it became very crossing. . . . Why should these things be given to me to bear to the world, and not to the learned, or to one of a different condition from myself?"

From a human viewpoint, the prospect must have been terrifying and well-nigh overwhelming; but "with God all things are possible" (Matt. 19:26).

NOTES

[1] William Foy, *The Christian Experience of William E. Foy Together With the Two Visions He Received in the Months of January and February 1842* (Portland, Me.: The Pearson Brothers, 1845), p. 21.

[2] Ellen G. White, *The Southern Work* (Washington, D.C.: Review and Herald Pub. Assn., 1966), p. 4.

[3] Franklin, *From Slavery to Freedom,* p. 158.

[4] *Ibid.,* p. 160.

[5] Lerone Bennett, *Before the Mayflower: A History of the Negro in America* (New York: Penguin Books, 1966), p. 69.

[6] Sydney Ahlstrom, *A Religious History of the American People* (New Haven, Conn.: Yale University Press, 1972), p. 702.

[7] Franklin, pp. 160, 161.

[8] Peter M. Bergman, *Chronological History of the Negro in America* (New York: New American Library), p. 138.

[9] Franklin, p. 161.

[10] *Ibid.,* pp. 61, 62.

[11] Bennett, p. 153.

[12] *Ibid.,* p. 153.

[13] *Ibid.,* pp. 153, 154.

[14] Franklin, p. 179.

The spirit of revivalism in the 1800s affected a wide group of people—regardless of race and culture.

CONVERSION

"As the deer pants for the water brooks, so pants my soul for You, O God.
My soul thirsts for God, for the living God. When shall I come and appear before God?"

Psalm 42:1, 2, NKJV

Silas Curtis, a prominent minister in the Freewill Baptist Church, baptized Foy in 1835 when he was 17 years of age. Line engraving made in the late 1800s.

A Spiritual Father and Example

We are indebted to Foy himself for the story of his personal conversion experience. He describes it in his pamphlet *The Christian Experience of William E. Foy Together With the Two Visions He Received in the Months of January and February, 1842.*

Foy begins by telling us how he met Jesus and came to have a personal relationship with Him. His testimony was helpful to Christians then, and it can be helpful to Christians today. Foy says,

"In the year 1835, under the preaching of Elder Silas Curtis, I was led to inquire what I should do to be saved." [1]

At the time of his conversion Foy was 17. Silas Curtis not only presented Christ to the young Foy but became his spiritual friend and example. Foy always looked back to this encounter as a turning point in his life. Silas Curtis was pastoring at the Freewill Baptist church in Augusta, where Foy lived at the time. The Freewill Baptist church was not far away, and since Blacks were encouraged to become members, it was not unusual that Foy would attend services there.

Who was Silas Curtis? What was there about him and his experience that caused Foy to inquire, like the jailer in Acts, "What must I do to be saved?"

To Foy's contemporaries the name of Silas Curtis held special significance, especially in Maine, where he had a long and influential ministry. Curtis was born in Auburn (then Minot), Maine, on February 27, 1804. Having secured an education in the local schools of the area, he prepared for college in the Maine Wesleyan Seminary at Kent's Hill, but his health was impaired, so he never entered college. He was converted in 1820, when nearly 17 years of age, and was baptized in May of the following year. At the age of 21 he began teaching school, and continued for some six years. In the spring of 1827, at age 23, he also began to preach the gospel. Curtis was ordained that same year to the Freewill Baptist Church ministry. During the next three or four years he preached in a number of towns in northern Maine. It was said that revivals of great power attended his labors.

In 1831 Curtis married Patience Gould, of Wayne, Maine. The couple settled in Monmouth for a short time. He spent the summer of 1833 in Providence, Rhode Island, then moved on to the pastorate of the church in Augusta, Maine, where he remained five years. From Augusta he moved to Lynn, Massachusetts, but finding that the ocean air did not agree with his health, he became pastor of the Lowell, Massachusetts, church (while there he lost his only child). From that point he moved on to several other successful pastorates. He died in the city of Concord, Maine, on April 23, 1880. It was said of him that "the burden of his fourscore and four years are upon him, and with true love for his people he awaits the great change which will bring to him again the friends of his early ministry in the better land."[2]

William Foy later became a pastor in the same denomination, and no doubt Silas Curtis's ministry was a source of encouragement to him. Silas Curtis's record was an exemplary one. During his ministry he was said to have baptized 800 converts, assisted in organizing several churches, and preached at the dedication of 12 church edifices. Besides his long and fruitful ministry, he was conspicuously active and influential in every denominational enterprise. His name is quickly obvious to even the cursory student of Freewill Baptist history. He was one of the foremost among those who began a new era of progress among his people by the publication of the paper *The Morning Star,* which spoke courageously on behalf of the antislavery movement. He was also involved in the founding of educational institutions and the organization of benevolent societies.

In addition to his religious calling, Silas Curtis was actively involved in the antislavery movement. The Freewill Baptist Church provided a pulpit for him to preach, teach, and write against slavery. Historically, Freewill Baptists were active against slavery and took the forefront in promoting the cause of Blacks. Shortly after 1830, when William Lloyd Garrison made his famous demand, "Immediate emancipation is the right of the slave and the duty of the master," Freewill Baptists took a bold and unflinching position on the side of freedom. In 1834 a Freewill Baptist minister, John Chaney, introduced antislavery resolutions at the Freewill Baptist quarterly meeting in Farmington. It was reported that Silas Curtis traveled 40 miles to defend the resolutions, which were adopted with only one or two dissenting votes.[3]

In March 1835, at a yearly meeting in Lisbon, the Freewill Baptists could rightfully say that "while the first missionary-elect was ordained to bear the gospel to our darker-hued brothers in the jungles of India, those in the cotton and rice fields of our own country were not forgotten." In the same year, resolutions recommending immediate emancipation were adopted by congregations in Maine, Vermont, Rhode Island, and New York. The following October, at the general conference in Byron, New York, the following action was taken: "Resolved, that we have abundant cause for gratitude to God, that as a denomination we are . . . generally united in our views on this distracting subject of slavery."[4]

A preacher, Silas Curtis, and a church, the Freewill Baptists, felt constrained by God to act a small part in the downfall of the cruelest institution this country has ever embraced.

NOTES

[1] Foy, *Christian Experience,* p. 7.
[2] G. A. Burgess, *Free Baptist Cyclopedia,* p. 146.
[3] *Ibid.*
[4] *Ibid.,* p. 20.

Components of a Christian Experience

Young Foy was attracted by the power and forcefulness of biblical preaching and teaching. The convicting power of the Holy Spirit caused him to "inquire what I should do to be saved." But the benevolent and nondiscriminatory attitude of the Freewill Baptists allowed him to have opportunity to hear the gospel.

Foy's pamphlet of 24 pages focuses as much emphasis on his Christian experience as on his visions. He seems to want us to know that a spokesman for God does not operate in a vacuum. He does not just appear, with no beginning or ending. He is a person with feelings, doubts, trials, and triumphs. He wants us to understand his conversion experience, in order to have a context for the visions he records. Taking deliberate care, he paints the scenario for the revelations that immediately follow.

Though he may not have meant it as such, Foy's recounting of his conversion experience can serve as an outline of the basic steps in the conversion process. In this account we see the vulnerable candor of his literary style and gain insights into traits of his personality that surface later in his life and ministry.

"In the year 1835, under the preaching of Elder Silas Curtis, I was led to inquire what I should do to be saved. Christians directed me to the Lamb of God, that taketh away the sins of the

*world. I then began to pray earnestly to God to pardon my sins; but the more I prayed, the more I beheld the sinfulness of my heart; and for many days I feared there was no mercy for me; but was led to see that it would have been justice in God to have cut me off and sent me where hope or mercy could not have reached me. I then became willing to give up all; and in that moment Christ appeared the One altogether lovely, and the chiefest among ten thousands, and spake the life-giving word to my soul. I then rejoiced in the God of my salvation; while all things around me appeared new, shining forth with the glory of God. Then could my heart unite in the song of the angels, 'Glory to God in the highest, and on earth peace, good will toward men' (Luke 2:14). I then saw such a fullness in Christ that I wanted to proclaim it to all the world. O the glory of God that filled my soul! Three months rolled away in which I enjoyed sweet communion with my God. I was then thrown into a trial by those who should have been nursing fathers in Israel, and thus remained many days, struggling in prayer; but the Lord knows how to deliver the godly out of temptation. A father in Israel whom I visited at this time gave me instruction that proved a blessing to my soul. I then joined the Sabbath school, and was there instructed for the first time to read the Word of God, and soon became able to read my little Bible. Immediately the duty of baptism was impressed upon me; and after three months' disobedience, I went before the church and related the dealings of God to my soul, and the day following was led down into the liquid stream by Brother S. Curtis, and was buried with my Saviour in baptism. Then did I experience the fulfillment of the promise: 'They that wait upon the Lord shall renew their strength; they shall mount up with wings as eagles; they shall run, and not be weary; and they shall walk, and not faint' (Isa. 40:31); and while [I was] coming up out of the water, it appeared to me the opening heavens around me shone; and I cried with a loud voice, saying: 'Glory to God and the Lamb that sitteth upon the throne!'"**

When the preaching of the Word corresponded to Foy's

quest for salvation, he was ready to learn how the process might be accomplished. Fortunately, Christ was uplifted as the one who could deal effectively with the sin problem.

Freewill Baptists place great emphasis on the free, full gospel of grace for "whosoever will." This liberating gospel, available to any needy sinner, was especially good news to Blacks, who were excluded from many communions. Freewill Baptists were known to preach with burning utterances, showing men and women the wickedness and hopelessness of their ways. But they also stressed the Christian's hope by showing that anyone, Black or White, male or female, could come to Christ and escape from the wrath to come.

Foy's natural response to his conversion experience was to tell others—to give to others what he himself had received. Granted, at that time he didn't have much religious instruction, and this lack apparently was the reason for a trial of faith that he soon experienced. But he did know what Christ had done for him, and he knew that if Christ could do something for him He could do it for others as well. These and other thoughts doubtless motivated him. Christ, His glory, His grace, and His goodness were the things that Foy wanted to tell others about. "Let your light so shine before men, that they may see your good works, and glorify your Father which is in heaven" (Matt. 5:16).

NOTE

* Foy, *Christian Experience,* pp. 7-9.

The African Meeting House was built by free Blacks on Beacon Hill not far from where Foy lived on Grove Street. It is one of the oldest standing Black church buildings in the United States. It was constructed to function as both a religious and an educational community center.

A Season of Trial

Trials were Foy's postconversion introduction to the Christian life. But these very trials helped him to see more clearly God's will. His testimony to the church was the outgrowth of this experience, which led triumphantly to his baptism. Let's look at the record Foy leaves of his trial:

"I was then thrown into a trial by those who should have been nursing fathers in Israel, and thus remained many days, struggling in prayer; but the Lord knows how to deliver the godly out of temptation." [1]

What was the trial that proved to be so vexing that he struggled in prayer many days? Foy had specifically stated his overwhelming desire to proclaim to the world what God had done for him. Three months after his conversion he talked about enjoying sweet communion with God. It appears that as he settled into his relationship with Christ he also settled into his conviction to enter the ministry.

Apparently the church leaders who might have encouraged him in his aims for the ministry sought to dissuade him. As a result, he said he was greatly discouraged. Needing encouragement and guidance but receiving none brought on a great spiritual dilemma. Prayer was the way by which he sought to find answers. He calls the whole experience a temptation and admits wrestling with it for many days. Then he reaches a conclusion—one that seemed to give him great satisfaction and contentment. He quotes 2 Peter 2:9, "The Lord knoweth how to deliver the godly out of temptations," and then explains how God effected his deliverance.

He providentially found the answer to his dilemma when visiting with a wise and mature church member. Foy apparently tells his friend about his experience and his great desire to tell others about what Christ has done for him. He wants to be a minister. He also tells him of the opposition he received and that this is a major trial to him. The counsel he received encouraged him to pursue further instruction and training and to let God lead him from that point on.

Taking this advice, Foy joins the Sabbath school (what today is called Sunday school). At that time it was a Bible class, widely used by most Protestant churches to teach and instruct the believer in a variety of spiritual skills—Bible doctrines, witnessing, tract distribution, etc.

Thus Foy was instructed for the first time in Christian doctrine and also in the art of Bible reading. He had never received this in-depth training before, and felt it was a blessed answer to his prayer. Soon he was reading his own Bible. The thoroughness of his training is attested to by the fact that throughout his writings there are numerous references to the Scriptures. In this setting he also received the instruction necessary to help prepare him for the ministry.

We are not told how long Foy attended the training classes, but he tells us that after approximately three months he was impressed to be baptized. For three months he had avoided baptism and called himself disobedient. Shortly thereafter, Foy did submit to the direction of the Word and was baptized.

Prior to baptism he went before the church to testify of his experience. This took courage, for in the average mixed congregation of the day, even in the Freewill Baptist Church, Blacks were not particularly welcome "up front." The Christian philosophy of equality only bent the color line; it did not break it. Just because Blacks were members of a church did not assure their equal participation. freemen, like slaves, were usually assigned seats in the back rows, and denied most rights of church membership.

So Foy's witness required unusual resolve. He records that he told his fellow members of the dealings of God with his soul. He told of his whole experience—his conversion, his trials, his breakthrough, and quite probably his determination for the ministry. Once Foy decided to be baptized and had delivered his testimony, there was no hesitation. He quickly and joyfully fulfilled the command of his Lord.

Foy concludes his account of conversion and baptism by stating: "While coming up out of the water, it appeared to me the opening heavens around me shone." He had an exhilarating panoramic view of heaven as if it were opening with an engulfing brilliance. In spontaneous response, he "cried with a loud voice, saying: 'Glory to God, and the Lamb that sitteth upon the throne!'"[2]

Foy leaves with us this rapturous scene as he concludes his opening record. The context is established; the stage is set. He has met the Lord. He has accepted his commission to minister. He has been blessed with God's presence.

After his baptism, the next incident he refers to is in Boston, seven years later, in 1842. But before we go there, let's piece together some of the ensuing events that took place in his life. Using city directories, census records, and other various documents, we can put together an adequate sketch of Foy's life during those seven years.

NOTES

[1] Foy, *Christian Experience*, p. 8.
[2] *Ibid.*, pp. 8, 9.

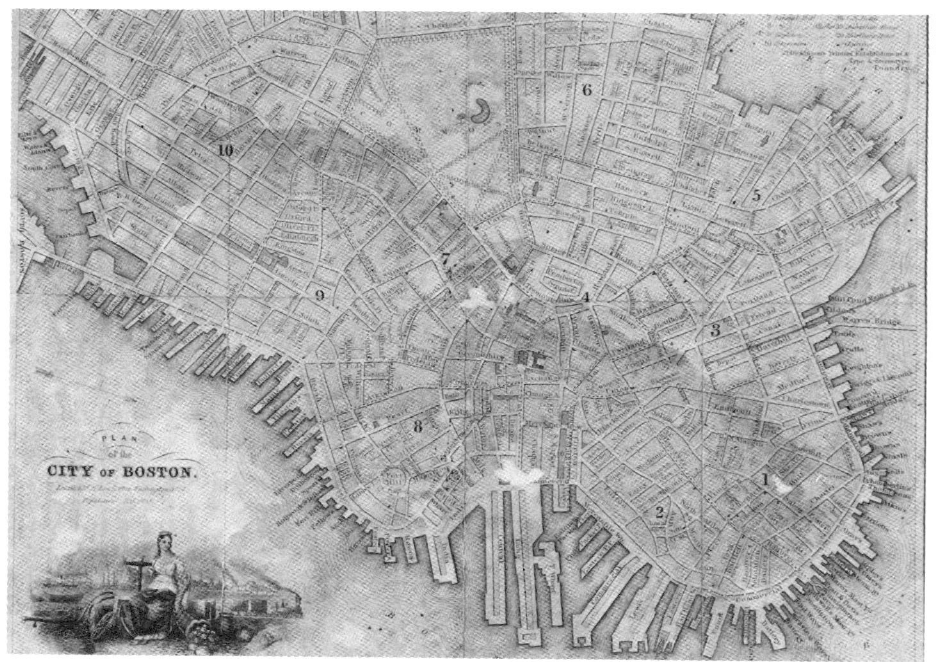

Map of the city of Boston as it looked in 1843. Beacon Hill and the other streets referred to by Foy can be found in Section 6.

CONNECTIONS

"There was also interest at this time in starting a special drive to warn American Blacks of the coming Advent. . . . There was a very practical problem, however: most of America's Blacks lived as slaves in the Southern states, and the abolitionist beliefs of the majority of Millerite lecturers made them personae non grata *in the South."*

Richard Schwarz
Light Bearers to the Remnant, *p. 45*

PEOPLE OF COLOR.

—

AKINS JOHN, waiter, Peck lane
Alexander Solomon, housewright, h. 2 Belknap
Alexander S. R. housewright, h. 2 Belknap
Allen Jesse, laborer, h. W. Centre cor. Southac
Alley William, hairdresser, near 494 Washington
Alves Francis, laborer, h. W. Cedar cor. May
Atkins Dean, mariner, h. Robinson lane
Avory Peter, hairdresser, Chambers cor. Poplar

BARBADOES ISAAC, h. Holden place
Barton John, mariner, Hanover avenue
Bassett Benj. P. hairdresser, 33 Endicott, h. 26 Belknap
Battiest Charles, boarding, h. 4 Sun court
Bell F. L. tailoress, h. Southac place
Bell John M. h. 12 Belknap
Bell William, laborer, h. Southac place
Beman Jehiel, h. 13 North Grove
Benjamin Catharine, widow of Samuel, h. 9 Fruit
Biner Charles, teamster, S. May near Washington
Black George H. Rev. h. 8 Belknap near Cambridge
Black Leonard, clothes cleaner, 46 Congress, h. Belknap
Bradford George, h. rear 29 Belknap
Brewster John, laborer, h. rear May
Brooks John, Peck lane
Brown John, h. rear 29 Belknap
Brown John, h. Grove
Brown Robert R. mariner, h. rear 147 Ann
Brown Thos. waiter, Atkinson, n. Milk, h. W. Centre
Brown William, waiter, h. 28 Belknap

Burr James, waiter, h. 28 Belknap
Burr Lemuel, hairdresser, 62 Court
Burrill Susan, widow, h. Southac court
Bush Alice, widow, 31 South Russell
Butler J. W. waiter, Atkinson n. Milk, h. 12 Fruit

CÆSAR ELI, barber, 117 Broad, h. 1 Butolph
Carpenter Henry, clothes, 24 Brattle, h. 18 Belknap
Carroll William, laborer, h. Cyprus
Carter James, clothes repairer, 74 Cambridge
Cash Jonathan, handcartman, h. 103 Chambers
Chadwick Elvin, barber, 99 Hanover, h. Southac
Christian James, clothing, 151 Ann
Clark Anthony F. (*Putman & C.*), h. 12 Belknap
Clarke Jonas W. clothes dealer, h. May
Clary George C. hairdresser, Broad near Forthill wharf,
   h. rear Southac
Clash Joseph F. barber, 183 Hanover, h. rear 152 Ann
Coburn John P. clothes dealer, 8 Brattle, h. Southac
Coburn Lewis, hairdresser, h. Southac place
Coburn Smith, teamster, h. Robinson lane
Cole Samuel, boarding, 2 Richmond
Cole Thomas, hairdresser, 3 Atkinson, h. Southac ct.
Cook Samuel S. hairdresser, h. Derne op. Ridgeway lane
Cooper Thomas, h. Southac c. W. Centre
Coston William, mariner, h. rear 157 Ann
Cummings Thomas, laborer, h. rear Charles near Chesnut

DALTON THOMAS, waiter, h. 29 S. Russell
Davis Henry, laborer, h. Southac
Davison Cæsar, h. Butolph
Dewitt Alexander, hairdresser, 39 Leveret
Dimorist Francis, hairdresser, 142 Com'l, h. 6 Southac ct.
Drummond Thomas, boarding, 245 Ann
Durfy William, laborer, h. Southac

ELI JOHN, clothes, 38 Brattle, h. rear 4 Southac
Emery Henry, waiter, h. South pl.

FENNOW WILLIAM, mariner, h. rear 7 Prince
Ferguson Moses, laborer, h. 3 Southac ct.
Fisher Jacob, mariner, 53 Spring
Foreman Henry, boarding, 157 Ann
Foster Cyrus, h. Southac place
Foy William, h. 16 N. Grove

The 1841 Boston Directory. Foy is the last name listed on page 483 and resided in house (h) 16 on North Grove. See Grove Street on map at beginning of Section 3.

Transition: Augusta to Boston

In the published account of his Christian experience and visions, seven years elapse between Foy's baptism and his first vision in Boston. While he may have felt these years were peripheral to the main purpose for writing his pamphlet (the details he supplied simply facilitated the presenting of his experience with the objective "to comfort of the saints"), it is helpful for us to have an idea of what transpired during those years. Where did he go? What did he do, and why? What were the conditions he faced? The answers to these questions can give us an understanding of his reason for being in Boston.

Direct information concerning this time in Foy's life is especially skimpy. Therefore, the period must be reconstructed from other available sources. For example, in the latter part of his pamphlet Foy tells us that when he felt his "family would come to want," he went to work laboring with his hands. We can assume three things immediately. One, he had little money at the time he felt this. Two, he had a family at that time. Three, he had and used a trade. Such details are more relevant when combined with other information, such as how he and his parents earned a living when he was growing up.

It should be remembered that we face a genealogical problem in searching out finer details about a Black person. We are fortunate that so much heretofore undiscovered information has surfaced concerning Foy, but the limitations are still real. As James Horton appropriately says in his scholarly work *Black Bostonians*: "It is especially difficult to study poor, working-class people in the nineteenth century, and even more difficult when they are Black."

But let us move on to what we do know concerning some of the domestic aspects of William Foy's life.

Foy was baptized in the Freewill Baptist church in Augusta and maintained his membership there. Later, when publishing his pamphlet, he included a reproduction of the text of his certificate of church membership. Foy always considered this connection with his first congregation family a point of great importance. Indeed, it was the focal point of his acceptance, the trial ground of his practice of the basics of the Christian life. His experience here prepared him for his later experiences.

Foy's marriage probably took place in 1836, the year after his conversion, though no record of his marriage is on file (this omission was also common during these times).

Ellen White refers to his wife. She mentioned that in one of the meetings she attended to hear Foy speak, she sat by his wife.[1] This took place in the early 1840s in the Portland area, so presumably it was Ann Foy, his first wife, mentioned at the back of his pamphlet.

Ellen White said that when Foy was speaking, his wife was "anxious," "sat looking at him," and "kept moving about." Foy, in turn, would tell her to relax, that there was no reason to be so nervous. Why did she act in this manner? Ellen White said she found out the reason for Mrs. Foy's actions after the meeting, when Foy went to where she was sitting, but Ellen White did not elaborate. One suggestion is that not only was Foy under pressure when he spoke, but his wife was also, and she showed her anxiety and nervousness by her movement. Apparently, she feared for his safety in his public roles before Whites as well as Blacks. Such a reaction is understandable when one considers the tensions between races, and the reaction to one relating visions, during that period.

There are indications that in 1837, a year or so after their marriage, the Foys had a baby girl, whom they named Amelia. A 23-year-old person named Amelia appears in the 1860 census record as living with Foy and his mother in Brunswick, Maine. Apparently by that time Ann Foy and Foy's father had died.

So in the late 1830s Foy appears to be living in the Augusta area with his wife and baby. But uppermost in his mind is the desire to prepare for and enter the gospel ministry. As there were few better places to prepare for such a work than in Boston, Foy moved there about 1840.

Boston holds a significant place in the history of the United States, for it was the seedbed of a variety of reforms and social movements that affected all other parts of the nation. Particularly important is Boston to our study because many events that happened there had an impact on William Foy's life. And it was there that Foy received his visions.

Boston was a city preeminently rich in a most appealing attraction: its ethnic composition. All races, classes, and cultures walked its streets, spoke in its halls, and associated on its wharves.

The Millerite movement centered its activities in Boston, only a few blocks from where Foy lived, had his visions, and later related them. On October 14, 1840, the Millerites held their first general conference of Adventist believers at the Chardon Street Chapel. On Wednesday morning Joshua V. Himes, the officiating pastor of the church, opened the conference with the following call: "The undersigned, believers in the second coming and kingdom of the Messiah 'at hand,' cordially unite in the call of a general conference of our brethren of the United States and elsewhere, who are also looking for the Advent near, to meet at Boston, Massachusetts, October 14, 1840, at 10:00 a.m., to continue two days, or as long as may then be found best. The object of the conference will not be to form a new organization in the faith of Christ; not to assail others of our brethren who differ from us in regard to the period and manner of the advent; but to discuss the whole subject faithfully and fairly, in the exercise of that spirit of Christ in which it will be safe immediately to meet Him at the judgment seat. By so doing we may accomplish much in the rapid, general, and powerful spread of 'the everlasting gospel of the kingdom' at hand, that the way of the Lord may be speedily prepared, whatever may be the precise period of His coming."[2]

So Boston was an important place to be at this time, an appropriate place for God to give special revelations for His people. What drew William Foy to this particular city? To answer this question, we must examine the Boston in which Foy lived and worked.

Boston was a study in paradoxes. On the one hand, the city was a champion of freedom and human rights, the birthplace of freedom for Blacks. On the other hand, it was steeped in segregation and inequity, a situation probably best exhibited in the matter of housing.

Foy moved into 16 North Grove Street, an inauspicious dwelling place, small and modest, in the Beacon Hill area. Beacon Hill was conveniently located in a northeastern section of Boston, and was in easy walking distance to just about any location in the city.[3] To illustrate, let us take a few key locations and measure the distance between them.

Remember that Foy lived on North Grove. Southark (Southock) Street, where Foy had his first vision, intersected with Grove Street about one block away. May Street, where he had his second vision, also intersected with Grove Street, about a block in the other direction. Those who testified to have witnessed Foy in vision lived within two or three blocks of where he lived and had his visions. The one exception is the doctor who examined him; he lived to the far northeast of Beacon Hill.

To reach Chardon Street Chapel, the meeting place of the Millerites, one would turn right off Grove, go 10 blocks down, and veer to the left. Broomfield (Bromfield) Street, where Foy first related his visions, was to the southeast of Grove Street, approximately 14 blocks away. This was probably the furthest of the sites under discussion.

The Boston community was so laid out that points of importance were in close proximity. Parts of the district are still as they were during Foy's time. Small narrow streets wind up the steep hill, with houses on both sides fitted compactly together. By 1860 almost two thirds of the city's Blacks lived on Beacon Hill. The lower slopes of the Hill were thought of as solidly Black, but this was not true. Even in the most segregated areas, Blacks and Whites lived adjacent to each other or at times even shared the same dwellings.

Probably the strongest attraction to Boston for Foy was the schools. Here were to be found excellent educational opportunities for a freeman, because many educational reforms had actually originated in Boston. Consequently, Blacks in the city of Boston were quite literate for that period of time. The city records reveal the following: "In 1850 the census reported that only 14 percent of the city's Black adults were unable to read and write. By 1860 the number of Blacks who were illiterate had dropped to 8 percent. Massachusetts-born Blacks were least likely to be illiterate, reflecting the concern for public education within the state. Northern-born Blacks were far more likely to have basic reading and writing skills than Southern-born Blacks. As might be expected, illiteracy was highest among the lowest skilled workers." [4]

However, that fact should be balanced by the following consideration: "It would be misleading to assume that literacy in the mid-nineteenth century meant anything more than a rudimentary knowledge of reading and writing. Many of those judged literate were, in fact, functional illiterates, able to write little more than their names, and, in some cases, unable to read and comprehend a newspaper."[5]

Even so, many Blacks, including Foy, evidently found Boston to be an ideal place to educate themselves. John Loughborough later referred to him as an educated and eloquent speaker.

What was religious life like for Blacks in Boston? That question can best be answered by surveying how the Black churches came about and noting three well-known Black preachers in the Boston of Foy's day.

BLACK POPULATION OF BOSTON, 1830-1860

Year	Total Population of Boston (thousands)	Black Population	% of Total Population
1830	61.4	1,875	3.1
1840	84.4	1,988	2.4
1850	136.9	1,999	1.5
1860	177.8	2,261	1.3

SOURCE: Peter R. Knights, *Plain People of Boston, 1830-1860* (New York, 1971), p. 29.

"The Black church arose in Boston partly as a response to the discrimination faced by Blacks in White churches and partly in response to the needs for self-expression which originated in the culture and experience of the Black community."[6] For the most part, Northern churches practiced segregation, though more subtly than the Southern ones. However, it should be noted that this did not include all churches. Many of the White and Black believers, especially Advent believers, practiced integration.

Ongoing discrimination caused the withdrawal of many Blacks from White churches, providing impetus for the formation of Black churches. In the 1800s small pockets of Blacks met for worship in private homes—their private protest against discrimination. Three ministers were a part of this evolution. Two of the three knew William Foy.

First, there was Thomas Paul. Baptized at the age of 16 in Exeter, New Hampshire, Paul assumed the role of an exhorter, explaining Scripture passages to the congregation in an informal setting. By the time he was 31 years old, he had a growing group of worshipers. He returned to New Hampshire on May 1, 1805, to be ordained. When he returned to Boston, he set about to formally organize the first Black church, the African Baptist church.

In 1829, because of poor health and the increasing demands of a growing membership, Thomas Paul resigned. Following his resignation, a number of interim and short-term pastors led the African Baptist church. Finally in 1840, 46 members, led by George Black, left to form a new church, which later became the Twelfth Baptist church on Southack Street. It was in a meeting at this church that Foy received his first vision. Foy refers to George Black in his second vision.

Finally, there was Samuel Snowden, the pastor of the growing and enthusiastic African Methodist Episcopal church on May Street on Beacon Hill. This was the site of Foy's second vision.

Snowden, along with many in his congregation, made forthright attacks on slavery. Their efforts to "improve the lives of local Blacks, most notably Black seamen, attracted many Black activists to his church. David Walker, the outspoken Black abolitionist and writer, was not only a member of Snowden's congregation but was also a personal friend of Sammy Snowden."[7] "Snowden's church attracted not only activists but the unskilled and fugitive slaves as well. Like both Baptist churches in Boston during the 1840s and 1850s, the AME church was a stop on the underground railroad." [8]

Preparation for the future required means for today, so for Foy the condition of Boston's job market was a primary consideration. Blacks performed a variety of jobs. Some were unskilled laborers; others were construction helpers or stevedores. Many became domestics (cooks, maids, butlers, and coachmen). Others worked as tradesmen, sailmakers, caterers, barbers, tailors, seamstresses, blacksmiths, printers, shoemakers, masons, bakers, musicians, seamen, and gardeners.

"At the top of the Black occupational scale stood a very few professionals—doctors, ministers, teachers, and lawyers. Their numbers were minuscule, and although there was a steady growth in this class, their percentage of the city's total Black work force ranged from less than 1 percent in 1830 to about 2 percent in 1860."[9]

For the most part, unskilled labor and low salaries were the norm for Black freemen. An often-times distressing situation faced a Black as he confronted the economic reality of providing for a family while obtaining an education. But Boston offered Foy a relatively good opportunity to secure a livelihood and prepare for his future labors.

Boston was a fertile ground for protest and political organization movements. Here Foy must have been personally exposed to various protest movements. His sensitivity to causes is evident in his awareness of various issues, concerns, and prejudices. Boston's unique persona allowed for positive social change and explosive social reaction. But the issue of issues— a social concern already of national proportions in Foy's day— was the slavery question.

What was family life like in the mid-1800s for Black families? Generally they lived in homes they did not own. Four people comprised an average Black household—a married couple and two children. Households sometimes included extended family relations—aunts, uncles, and in-laws. Black families were seldom isolated. Most lived multiple-family style, with all the attendant advantages and problems. Boarding can be traced back to custom as well as to economic and social necessity. As Blacks were excluded from the city's hotels and from most White boardinghouses, Black boarders stayed in Black-operated boardinghouses, which were few. Lodging was found most often in rented rooms in Black households.[10]

Foy arrived in Boston at one of its most turbulent and historic periods. He was caught up in the history of the period. God picked him to be the recipient of the gift of prophecy during a time when people were most sensitive to the divine countdown of Providence.

NOTES

[1] Ellen White, "William Foy—A Statement by E. G. White," E. G. White Estate Document File 231.

[2] Isaac C. Wellcome, *History of the Second Advent Message and Mission, Doctrine, and People* (New York: A. A. Phelps, 1874), p. 177.

[3] See appendix C, Boston city map.

[4] James Horton, *Black Bostonians* (New York: Holmes and Meier, 1979), p. 12.

[5] *Ibid.*, p. 13.

[6] *Ibid.*, p. 7.

[7] *Ibid.*, p. 10.

[8] *Ibid.*, p. 13.

[9] *Ibid.*, p. 10.

[10] *Ibid.*, p. 16.

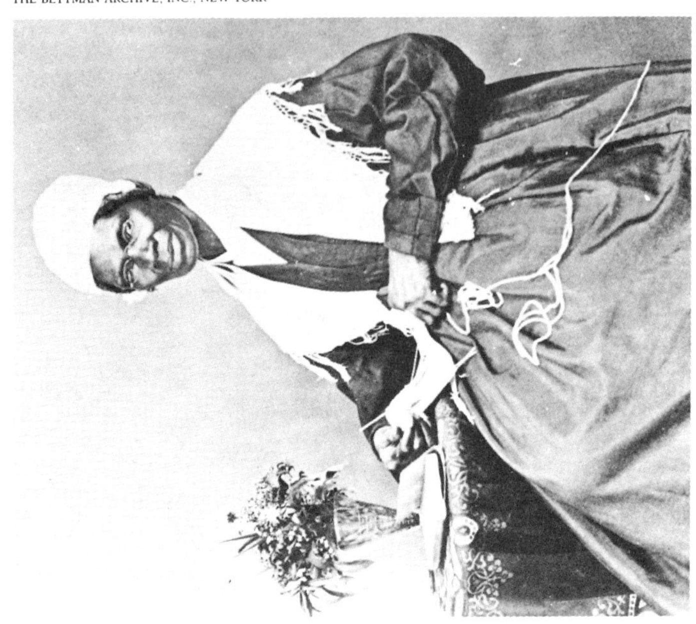

Sojourner Truth, a contemporary of Foy, was leader of the Underground Railroad movement, a believer in the Advent teachings, and one who frequented Millerite camp meetings.

William Miller, leader of the Advent movement, was sympathetic to Black concerns and endorsed Blacks joining the Millerite movement.

The Millerite Connection

William Foy had a consuming interest in the Second Advent. Further, the proximity of his house to a number of the historical Advent landmarks (i.e., Joshua V. Himes's church, the Advent printing press, etc.) in Boston regularly exposed him to Advent influences. Though Foy doesn't specifically mention his connection with the Millerites, he was obviously influenced by them—reference to the Advent and similar Millerite teachings is woven throughout his pamphlet. What can be constructed as to Foy's relation to the Millerites? And what was the Millerites' relation to Blacks in general?

Near the conclusion of his pamphlet, Foy speaks of a shift in his religious views. Speaking of his desire that the visions would comfort others as they comforted him, he went on to say,

"I am now awaiting for my coming Lord. Although before the Lord was pleased to show me these heavenly things, I was opposed to the doctrine of Jesus' near approach, I am now looking for that event." [1]

Foy didn't say he was opposed to the advent of Christ, but to His near advent. It seemed as though his thinking changed after receiving the visions. Because of the strength of his conviction, the Great Disappointment failed to greatly alter his views. The year after the Disappointment found him still looking to see his Lord very soon. And if he didn't see Christ during his lifetime? "Then 'I shall be satisfied,'" he responds, "'when I awake, with [His] likeness' (Ps. 17:15)."

Evidently, then, Foy became a believer in the Millerite message after receiving visions. The *Seventh-day Adventist Encyclopedia* bears out the fact that "after the visions he joined the Millerites in heralding the message of the expectation of Christ's soon coming."[2] Upon arriving in Boston, Foy apparently was aware of the Advent movement but not yet a part of it.

With time passing rapidly and the expected date of Christ's arrival just ahead, there was a need on the part of the Adventists for a brief but definite statement of their beliefs, especially in reference to the event soon to take place. Near the end of 1842 William Miller responded by issuing a synopsis of his views. Here are reproduced the beliefs, in Miller's words, that challenged Foy and thousands of others to anticipate an imminent Second Advent.

1. I believe Jesus Christ will come again to this earth.

2. I believe He will come in all the glory of His Father.

3. I believe He will come in the clouds of heaven.

4. I believe He will then receive His kingdom, which will be eternal.

5. I believe the saints will then possess the kingdom forever.

6. I believe at Christ's second coming the body of every departed saint will be raised, like Christ's glorious body.

7. I believe that the righteous who are living on the earth when He comes will be changed from mortal to immortal bodies, and, with them who are raised from the dead, will be caught up to meet the Lord in the air, and so be forever with the Lord.

8. I believe the saints will then be presented to God blameless, without spot or wrinkle, in love.

9. I believe, when Christ comes the second time, He will come to finish the controversy of Zion, to deliver His children from all bondage, to conquer their last enemy, and to deliver them from the power of the tempter, which is the devil.

10. I believe that when Christ comes, He will destroy the bodies of the living wicked by fire, as those of the old world were destroyed by water, and shut up their souls in the pit of woe, until their resurrection unto damnation.

11. I believe, when the earth is cleansed by fire, that Christ and His saints will then take possession of the earth, and dwell therein forever. Then the kingdom will be given to the saints.

12. I believe the time is appointed of God when these things shall be accomplished.

13. I believe God has revealed the time.

14. I believe many who are professors and preachers will never believe or know the time until it comes upon them.

15. I believe the wise, they who are to shine as the brightness of the firmament, will understand the time.

16. I believe the time can be known by all who desire to understand and to be ready for His coming. And I am fully convinced that sometime between March 21, 1843, and March 21, 1844, according to the Jewish mode of computation of time, Christ will come, and bring all

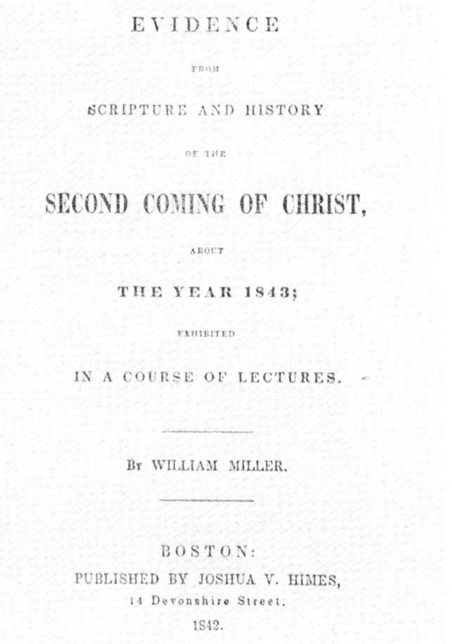

EVIDENCE

FROM

SCRIPTURE AND HISTORY

OF THE

SECOND COMING OF CHRIST,

ABOUT

THE YEAR 1843;

EXHIBITED

IN A COURSE OF LECTURES.

By WILLIAM MILLER.

BOSTON:
PUBLISHED BY JOSHUA V. HIMES,
14 Devonshire Street.
1842.

His saints with Him; and that then He will reward every man as his works shall be.[3]

God gave Foy a special revelation that convinced him of the reality of His coming, though not of the time. Throughout Foy's visions one catches a forceful sense of the reality of Christ's coming, but never is there suggested a time or date. In fact, if carefully studied, the visions indicate events that will transpire *before* Christ's return.

A definite and traceable connection existed between the concerns and interests of Blacks and those of the Millerite movement. A careful look at the life of William Foy will highlight this reality. In many historical accounts the early Advent movement seems to be barren of any substantial Black interest, and Millerite Adventists seemed oblivious to the legitimate spiritual and social concerns of Blacks. This, however, is not the case. A balanced handling of the subject should promote a better understanding of the relation of Blacks to the early beginnings of the Seventh-day Adventist Church. Further, it would show the breadth and broad-mindedness of Adventist pioneers, and this would offset the view that God was and is partial in His dealings. A focus on Black Millerite racial concerns might provide fundamental and substantive support for positive church race relations today.

The men who led the Millerite movement were just that— men, human beings! Though erring humans, they were interested in the great social issue of the day, the antislavery movement. However, with their minds focused on the doctrine of the Apocalypse, they could give only small attention to social activism.

Blacks too were vitally interested in and supportive of the spiritual concerns of the world to come. But they were temporally overwhelmed with the suffocating issues of slavery and injustice. The racial status quo stymied their ability to share fully in the movement, to present their views in a widespread manner.

Whether the Millerites would succeed or fail in the Black community depended to a great extent on their attitude toward slavery and abolition. Foy's concern with the effect of the color question on his God-given responsibility reflects the average Black's acute awareness of racial issues. If the Advent teaching was so heavenly minded that it was of no earthly good, then most Blacks would view it as impractical. Blacks at that time needed to see Christianity in action more than to hear it in theory. They needed to see men who believed that Bible principles affected and pervaded every area of life.

To the nineteenth-century Black church, religion was more than just a belief; it was an inextricable part of life, a way of coping with inequities, a way of realizing selfhood. "The history of Black Americans is closely bound up with the history of the Black church. For an oppressed and harassed people, religion provided a solace and a hope for better days to come in this life and in the eternal. For a people shut out of much of American society, with little hope of attaining position and prestige in traditional ways, the church performed many other functions as well." [4]

The Millerite movement was concerned with the salvation of Blacks and their more temporal concerns. Let us consider a few of the Blacks who were connected with the movement.

The Millerites didn't keep any significant records of Black participation in the movement for several reasons. First, they were terse; they didn't keep complete records on even their most prominent leaders. In his own brief summary of his life, William Miller covered the decade from 1830 to 1840 in three pages. Second, the Millerites weren't interested in keeping records because they saw themselves as leaving this world permanently in 1843 and thus had no need for records. Third, in spite of the Millerites being interracial in their proclamation, their major area of concentration was in New England, where there were fewer Blacks than in the South. Fourth, they knew that many Whites were inherently suspicious about Blacks being taught religion, especially about the Second Coming, which produced a liberating effect. Finally, records and histories of the movement that do exist were not chronicled in an organized manner; Millerite information comes primarily from their religious journals, newspapers, circulars, pamphlets, and broadsides, and these mention virtually nothing about race.

All of the Millerite Blacks that we have information on either originated in New England or spent a large portion of their lives there. Further, the Millerites drew the great majority of their adherents from the organized churches of the day, and the same was true among Blacks. Thus those Blacks who joined the Millerite movement came out of established Black churches. Primarily, these were the Baptist and Methodist churches because of their stand on abolition and because those were the churches in which most Blacks held membership.

Let us now look at a few of the Blacks who were connected in a public way with the Millerite movement.

The story of Charles Bowles, affectionately referred to as Father Bowles, is a fascinating one. He was born around the beginning of the nineteenth century in Boston. His father was an African servant and his mother was the daughter of the celebrated American Colonel Morgan, who fought in the Revolutionary War. At the early age of 14, Bowles enlisted in the Army and was servant to an officer. Though he felt a call to the ministry, he put it off by going to sea. However, in 1816 he entered the Freewill Baptist ministry, in Vermont. As fruit of his ministry there were 150 conversions, and a church of 90 members was raised up. He was ordained not long afterward.

Though he often met with bitter opposition because of his color, he became an effective and successful evangelist, with converts among Whites as well as Blacks. It is believed that he joined the Millerite movement as a result of attending one of their camp meetings. His preaching was much like that of the Millerite preachers of his day, using the standard Millerite exposition and explanation of prophecy.

On one occasion when a baptism was scheduled, he was threatened with being thrown into a pond. Instead of backing down, he continued to preach with such power that many of his tormentors were converted.

Father Bowles played a significant role in the Freewill Baptist Church as well as in the Millerite movement. He was instrumental in organizing quarterly meetings right up until his death in March 1843. His last sermon was preached on February 5 of that year, by which time he had become nearly blind. His funeral was marked by a large and solemn crowd.[5]

John Lewis was another Black Millerite minister who preached the prophecies of the soon return of Jesus. As a result of his preaching, a large number of Blacks faithfully awaited the Lord's return, and sadly were disappointed with the others in 1844. Following the Disappointment, they were scattered among the various groups that resulted. Elder Lewis, as he was called, wrote a biography on the life of Charles Bowles entitled *The Life, Labor, and Trials of Elder Charles Bowles of the Freewill Baptist Denomination*. As was the custom in that day, the title was further supplemented by an addendum: *Together With an Essay on the Character and Conditions of the Africans*.

These two ministers, along with William Foy, invested their efforts in the Millerite movement, working side by side with White preachers who heralded the coming of Christ.

Abolitionist and author of the well-known *Underground Railroad*, William Still was also an enthusiastic follower of William Miller and was a student of his prophecies on the coming of Christ. A native of Burlington County, New Jersey, Still was the son of Levin and Gidney Still, freemen who had purchased their freedom after being fugitives from a slave plantation in Maryland. Unable to secure an education in New Jersey because of abuse and persecution, Still later decided to strike out in new directions.

His experience is described in the following account: "By the next spring Still had a job as a farmhand at Evasham Mount and spent a year in this work. Then his father died, and young William, distraught and lonely, went into the wilderness to assess his own future and try to find God. By the middle of 1844, he had heard the preaching of William Miller, and, according to his memoirs in *Underground Railroad,* had found his answer: Christ *must* come back to the earth. There was no other hope. With this assurance he was ready for the disappointment and hardship of an unfriendly world."[6]

Black abolitionist, temperance reformer, and suffragette, Sojourner Truth was born in Hurley, New York, as Isabella (Baumfree) Van Wagener. Sojourner was freed under New York's gradual emancipation act in 1828. It is said that after a varied and difficult life, and convinced of divine direction, she walked out of New York City one day in 1843 with a bag of clothes, 25 cents, and a new name: Sojourner Truth. From that day until her death, she walked the land preaching, teaching, and lecturing. The *Seventh-day Adventist Encyclopedia* has this to say: "She set out for New England in 1843 to tell the people their sins, particularly the sin of slavery, and soon became the protégée of prominent New England abolitionist leaders. She was illiterate, but her ready wit, her quaint speech, and her commanding personality could captivate an audience. She could quell a crowd of hoodlums by singing or silence an opposer with sarcasm, as the case might require."[7]

Various stories have circulated about Sojourner, only some of which have been substantiated, but it is clear that she was aware of Advent teachings. She visited at least two of the Millerite camp meetings in 1843, one of which was in Connecticut.

Shortly after moving to Harmonia, Michigan, where she had friends, Sojourner moved some five miles to Battle Creek, "Where she enjoyed the friendship of John Byington, Dr. J. H. Kellogg, and other prominent SDAs."[8] There is a mixed opinion about her church status, but some sources favor the belief that she became a Seventh-day Adventist.

Sojourner Truth was buried in Battle Creek's Oak Hill Cemetery, where Ellen White is also buried. In her obituary, published in the old Adventist publication *Sunshine at Home,* by the Review and Herald Publishing Association in 1883, we read these words: "Her remains were deposited in Oak Hill Cemetery, there to await the return of the Life-giver, who will reward everyone according as his works have been."[9]

Thus, there are clear and strong connections between the Millerites and Blacks during the Advent movement. Also, it seems evident that Foy would have known these and other Blacks in the Millerite movement and that they would have known of him. So the influence of the Advent doctrine and Millerism on Foy was by no means unusual.

NOTES

[1] Foy, *Christian Experience,* p. 23.

[2] *Seventh-day Adventist Encyclopedia,* p. 474.

[3] James White, *Sketches of the Christian Life and Public Labors of William Miller* (Battle Creek, Mich.: SDA Pub. Assn., 1875), pp. 170-173.

[4] Horton, *Black Bostonians,* p. 39.

[5] John Lewis, *The Life, Labor, and Trials of Elder Charles Bowles.*

[6] *Ibid.*

[7] *Seventh-day Adventist Encyclopedia,* p. 1503.

[8] *Ibid.*

[9] *Sunshine at Home,* p. 92. Also referred to in the *Seventh-day Adventist Encyclopedia,* p. 1504.

24

TESTIMONIALS.

We, the undersigned, inhabitance of Boston, were witnesses of the apparently inanimate condition into which our brother, Wm. Ellis Foy, was thrown from some unknown cause, on the 18th of January 1842, when he laid two hours and a half; and again Febuary 4th, when he laid twelve hours and a half, during which, each time, he testifies that he experienced extraordinary visions of another world.

Charles Tash.	Francis Sanders.
George Williams.	John Thomas.
David Williams.	Andrew Lewis.
Edward Williams.	George Harris.

Dr. Henry Cummings, testifies: "I was present with our brother at the time of his visions. I examined him, but could not find any appearance of life, except around the heart."

Ann Foy testifies: "The first appearence of life I saw in him, was the raising of his right hand. He then arose upon his knees, and made signs for water, which was given him. He dipped his hand into it, and wet his forehead, and his speech immediately came to him. We then wished him to tell us, what things he had seen, and he answered, as soon as I receive strength, I will reveal unto you, that which the Lord has revealed unto me."

Copy of certificate of church membership.

This certifies that Bro. Wm. E. Foy, is a regular member, of the first Freewill Baptist Church, in Augusta, in good standing. And as such, we commend him to the fellowship of the people of God, of every name, wherever he may chance to meet them.

DANIEL PALMER,
Church Clerk.

The last page of Foy's pamphlet, The Christian Experience . . . , which contains a testimonial of Boston citizens who witnessed him in vision. Also seen is a copy of Foy's certificate of church membership.

COMMISSION

"With a lovely voice, the guide then spoke to me and said, 'Those that eat of the fruit of this tree return to earth no more.' I raised my hand to partake of the heavenly fruit, that I might no more return to earth; but alas! I immediately found myself again in this lonely vale of tears."

William E. Foy
Christian Experience, *p. 15*

A rare photograph of a New England camp meeting in the middle 1800s with Blacks shown sprinkled throughout the audience.

Preacher of Righteousness

Foy's aim was to be a preacher. Therefore, after being baptized by Silas Curtis, he and his family moved to Boston, where Foy could get the exposure needed to round out his ministerial training.

It was not unusual in Foy's day to see considerable intermingling among churches, so though he was a Baptist he aspired to ordination as an Episcopal minister.[1] Ellen White recalled his wearing an Episcopalian robe. In 1842, while Foy was in Boston, God gave him his first two visions, which he shared among Baptist and Methodist groups, respectively. Foy's first official account of what he had seen was to a Methodist congregation. In every likelihood both groups were believers in the near advent of Christ. Foy's espousal of Advent teachings wouldn't have affected his denominational standing as yet, as Millerites represented a variety of denominations. It was only later, in 1843, that the churches began to disfellowship Millerites.

What was Foy like as a preacher? What was the content, style, and effect of his preaching?

Prior to Foy's receiving visions, his preaching had much of the content of mainstream Protestantism in his day. With his Freewill Baptist background, he strongly emphasized free grace and the individual's choice in the matter of his salvation. He highlighted the mercy and grace of Christ, while stressing man's need for obedience and holy living. Of course, he made frequent reference to his personal experience of what Christ had done for him. Other important themes—such as Christ's perfect love, prayer, victory over temptation, Bible study, Christian fellowship, and baptism—no doubt surfaced in Foy's preaching.

Throughout his pamphlet he makes reference to these various truths. But he tells us that before he had his visions, he was opposed to the teaching of Jesus' near approach. After receiving the visions, however, his mind was changed. From then on, the second advent of Christ became an important subject of his preaching. Foy wanted to see Jesus! He wanted everyone to know of the joys that awaited the faithful. In addition, he stressed the physical return of Christ, the resurrection of the righteous, the destruction of the wicked, and the eternal redemption of the saints.

As mentioned earlier, there is no indication that Foy ever preached a specific date for the return of Christ. Many of the Millerite ministers were themselves unsure of an exact date; some prominent Millerites, like Henry Ward and Henry Jones, of New York City, actually were opposed to setting any definite time for the return of Christ.[2]

One cannot make a blanket statement to cover every Millerite Advent believer; the movement wasn't that homogeneous. But they united in that most cardinal Advent teaching—the personal, premillennial coming of Christ.

Though many saw danger in the preaching of even a definite year for the event, they believed the event to be near at hand. A comforting reality about the Millerite movement was that people of such divergent opinion could cooperate so heartily. This testified well to the Christian charity and broadmindedness of the movement, as well as to the unifying and consolidating influence of a shared belief in Christ's soon coming.

As to the content of Foy's preaching, there is yet a final and perhaps most significant aspect. That is the influence that the visions had on his preaching. Relating the visions became, in truth, an integral part of his sermonic presentations. His prophetic view of heaven as the home of the saved, varied aspects of the salvation process, the judgment, and numerous particulars concerning the Advent formed an extremely rich repertoire for preaching and teaching. Further, this was a time of revivals, and Foy contributed his share. His testimonies concerning the power and spiritual effect that accompanied his efforts are numerous.

Foy was "invited from place to place to speak in the pulpits, not by the Episcopalians only, but by the Baptists and other denominations."[3] J. N. Loughborough also noted that when Foy spoke, he wore the Episcopal clergyman's robe. Describing the effect of Foy's preaching, Loughborough records: "Mr. Foy's visions related to the near advent of Christ, the travels of the people of God to the heavenly city, the new earth, and the glories of the redeemed state. Having a good command of language, with fine descriptive powers, he created a sensation wherever he went. By invitation he went from city to city to tell of the wonderful things he had seen; and in order to accommodate the vast crowds who assembled to hear him, large halls were secured, where he related to thousands what had been shown him of the heavenly world, the loveliness of the New Jerusalem, and of the angelic hosts. When dwelling on the tender, compassionate love of Christ for poor sinners, he exhorted the unconverted to seek God, and scores responded to his tender entreaties."[4] Loughborough said Foy traveled through various parts of New England, preaching the Second Advent.

Foy wrote in his pamphlet, concerning the first time he related his visions, that the large congregation at Bromfield "sat in perfect stillness," obviously greatly impressed by what they'd heard. He went on to say that after that experience he delivered his message to crowded houses in many different places. Ellen White also spoke of Foy's travels and ministry. She said that she and her father went a number of times to hear Foy speak at Beethoven Hall, in Portland, Maine.

Loughborough makes this statement, capturing the mood of the times: "With such manifestations of the power of God in connection with the preaching of His coming 'at the doors,' and with the rejoicing of thousands who were turning from sin to serve the Lord, and to wait for His coming, the people were doubly assured that this was indeed the Lord's message to the world."[5]

Besides respecting Foy as a preacher, those who knew and heard him had a high view of the legitimacy of his revelatory experience. Of his contemporaries who made reference to his experience, none expressed any question concerning the veracity of his visions. Ellen White, after making reference to having heard him in person, said that he bore "remarkable testimonies."[6] And to John Loughborough, these "visions bore clear evidence of being the genuine manifestations of the Spirit of God."[7] In more recent years, Arthur White, custodian of Ellen White's writings, remarked, "I should judge from Loughborough's witness and from Ellen White's statement that Foy's experience was a genuine experience."[8]

The most complete statement on how Foy's experience was viewed was set forth by the Pearson brothers, the publishers of Foy's pamphlet. In the opening section of the pamphlet, entitled "Remarks," John and Henry Pearson expressed their confidence in these words: "The visions of our brother are certainly very remarkable, and when related by him in public assemblies, have been blessed by God to the awakening of sinners, reclaiming of backsliders, and the building of the saints in the most holy faith. They are published as nearly as possible in his own language. There is a most beautiful resemblance in the views here given with the visions of Ezekiel, Daniel, and John. As for instance, the description of the 'tall and mighty angel,' and 'the sea of glass.'"[9]

The Pearson brothers were well known in Advent circles and in the printing business. John was the editor of the short-lived journal *Hope of Israel,* in which appeared T. M. Preble's first discussion of the Sabbath. John was in partnership with his brother Henry until mid-1845. Sons of Father John Pearson, of Portland, Maine, both John and Henry were connected with the Adventist believers there. Their father was also connected with the early Adventists and later had interaction with Ellen White as well. A well-respected deacon in the Baptist Church, he initially had doubts about the reliability of visions in general and Ellen's experience in particular, but was later confirmed in their genuineness.

That the Pearsons printed and endorsed Foy's visions at that early time makes a significant statement. They knew that many people did not believe in the manifestation of dreams and visions. They fully accorded to such people their right to discern for themselves between true and false, yet they were clear in their conviction of the legitimacy of Foy's experience. And they set forth a strong argument concerning the legitimacy of visions.

They point out that "God does manifest Himself in vision to His children." He is not out of character when He does this. In fact, "the records of every age do abundantly testify"[10] to this. Further, the Bible explicitly validates visions, as in the cases of the patriarchs and prophets: Abraham (Gen. 15:1-17), Jacob (Gen. 28:12-15), Moses (Ex. 3:2; 24:9-11; 33:18-23), Joshua (Joshua 5:13-15), Isaiah (Isa. 6), Jeremiah (Jer. 1:11, 13), Ezekiel (Eze. 1:3-28), Daniel (Dan. 2). These men were shown, by the agency of visions, the great events yet to happen.

Did the use of divine manifestations stop when the "dispensation of the Spirit" began? The answer is no! Divine manifestations were evident during that period as well. The gospel age was ushered in with such distinct disclosures as that on the Mount of Transfiguration (Matt. 17:1-8). The Pearson brothers list several examples: Stephen (Acts 7:55, 56), Paul (Acts 9:3-6; 16:9; 18:9, 10; 22:17-21), John (Rev. 1:10-20ff.). They then pose a rhetorical question: "Tell me if Jehovah has ceased to reveal Himself in visions?"

God did promise to reveal Himself in the last days through the Spirit of prophecy (Joel 2:28). The Pearsons leave the reader to make his own conclusions, but as far as they were concerned, the case was clear and scripturally defensible. They did not publish Foy's visions as a polemic to try to convince people of the legitimacy of visions. Their object was "to comfort and encourage the dear saints of God in their weary pilgrimage." They saw this as being effected by giving weary Christians who had just experienced the Great Disappointment and were presently going through ridicule and derision "a glimpse of the blessedness awaiting the finally faithful."[11]

It is obvious that God blessed the efforts of William Foy as a preacher as well as a prophet and pioneer. But only eternity will show the full effects of his ministry.

NOTES

[1] John Loughborough, *The Great Second Advent Movement* (Washington, D.C.: Review and Herald Pub. Assn., 1905), p. 145.

[2] M. Ellsworth Olson, *A History of the Origin and Progress of the Seventh-day Adventists* (Washington, D.C.: Review and Herald Pub. Assn., 1925), p. 125.

[3] Loughborough, p. 145.

[4] *Ibid.,* p. 146.

[5] Loughborough, p. 147.

[6] Ellen White, "William Foy—A Statement by E. G. White."

[7] Loughborough, p. 146.

[8] Arthur White, letter, Mar. 1, 1959.

[9] Foy, *Christian Experience,* pp. 5, 6.

[10] *Ibid.,* p. 4.

[11] *Ibid.,* p. 3.

First Vision: Victory

Having overviewed William Foy and his times, we are ready now to consider the visions themselves. In his first vision Foy saw the early Advent movement—a movement not dying out in obscurity but going through a period of shaking, a movement being purified and led on to triumph. He saw the Advent saints ushered into the new earth, experiencing the glories and rewards that God has prepared for the faithful. The time span of his first vision extended from his day into the millennium.

Strong recurring themes characterize this vision and give it a particular tone. A strong emphasis is given to the following themes: 1. *Victory and triumph;* the vision shows that those who faithfully pass through the judgment will be granted eternal rewards—glorification and the partaking of heavenly bounties. 2. *Joy and happiness;* included in the vision are touching scenes of human interest, showing the inner jubilation experienced by the righteous. 3. *Regret and exclusion;* while not a dominant emphasis, this is resident throughout the entire depiction and appears twice, emphasizing the profound and eternal loss of those who did not make it to the New Jerusalem. 4. *Extension and delay;* this is implied in the content of the vision and in the fact that the events had not yet taken place. But this theme of delay is emphasized at the conclusion of the vision when Foy is told that the reward is not to be experienced yet.

According to Foy's visions, angels have an important role in the plan of redemption; he refers to angels more than 15 times. They are active in the affairs of men, interested in their salvation. The exhilaration of the saints—clad in glorious white raiment, wearing crowns, bearing cards—is echoed by that of the heavenly citizenry. Beautiful singing and joyful praise enliven the scene. The saints are placed in two categories— those who had passed through death and those who had not passed through death. Yet amid the scenes of joy a weight of sadness is keenly felt. There would be no mercy for the wicked because "they would not believe."

There is found in the visions a combination of biblical instruction and spiritual pathos that impressed and convicted Foy's hearers. We today are in a better position to see and understand the content of the visions and their possible meaning.

Our goal in studying these visions will be twofold. First, what message was God seeking to convey through the visions? And second, how were they received? This vision can be divided into 10 different scenes interspersed by what might be called interludes, when his guide spoke, and a final closing scene. But first let's look at the context in which he received his first vision.

"On the eighteenth of January, 1842, I met with the people of God in Southark Street, Boston, where the Christians were engaged in solemn prayer, and my soul was made happy in the love of God." [1]

The day was a Tuesday, the meeting place was on Southock Street, in the Beacon Hill area of Boston, several blocks from where Foy lived. As was his habit, he met with fellow Christians who regularly got together for exhortation and prayer. George Black, the individual Foy referred to in his second vision, was the pastor of this predominantly Black congregation.

The format of these meetings was simple and informal: prayer, singing, testifying, and sharing. Anyone, preacher or layman, could take the floor, read the Word, and expound on it. In this particular meeting Foy says that "the Christians were engaged in solemn prayer," and as a result, his "soul was made happy in the love of God."

His first visionary experience lasted two and a half hours and was witnessed by a Dr. Cummings; Ann Foy; and eight local citizens. His experience at the point of going into vision should sound somewhat familiar to Seventh-day Adventists: "I was immediately seized as in the agonies of death, and my breath left me; and it appeared to me that I was a spirit separate from this body."

Scene 1: *"I then beheld one arrayed in white raiment, whose countenance shone beyond the brightness of the stars."* [2]

He is introduced to an angelic guide, who would be with him in subsequent visions as well. The white raiment, radiant countenance, and bright crown of the heavenly inhabitant capture Foy's admiration and attention. It is obvious that Foy wants us also to be struck with the purity and holiness of this being. Foy developed a great trust in his guide.

Scene 2: *"This shining one took me by my right hand and led me upon the bank of a river."* [3]

In the middle of the river "was a mount of pure water." At this point, the river is the center of attention. On the bank is a multitude identified as the "living inhabitants" of the earth. All classes of people are included in this throng, men "both great and small." He makes a special note of the fact that of the people he saw, many were then still alive on the earth. His message thus had immediate impact on the hearers of his day.

Everyone begins to move to the "west, walking on the water," until they reach a raised level, a higher surface that he calls "the mount." Upon reaching it, the mixed multitude—the righteous and the wicked—is separated. The righteous cross the mount and experience three changes. The wicked, upon reaching the mount, find themselves unable to pass over. They cry out for mercy, then sink beneath the mount.

The west, the direction the group continues to move, seems to have had some special significance, for Foy refers to the west in his second vision as well. According to the *Seventh-day Adventist Dictionary,* the Hebrew word for west, *ma 'varab,* also means "sunset." [4] Possibly this movement toward the west symbolizes that this group is moving toward the sunset of history, toward the end of time.

The mount toward which the group moves brings to mind a judging, or testing—it is a separation point, even a terminal point for some in this multitude. That a mount might be a terminal point is suggested in Hebrews 12:18-24, which refers to the Israelites' gathering at Mount Sinai and the Christians' future meeting at Mount Zion: "For ye are not come unto the mount that might be touched, and that burned with fire, nor unto blackness, and darkness, and tempest; . . . but ye are come unto Mount Sion, and unto the city of the living God, the heavenly Jerusalem, and to an innumerable company of angels, to the general assembly and church of the firstborn, which are written in heaven, and to God the Judge of all."

Having safely crossed the mount, the righteous pass through "three changes." These three changes refer perhaps to the changes that take place at the second coming of Christ, when the glorification of the saints shall take place.

The first change was that "their bodies were made glorious." In 1 Corinthians 15:51, 52 Paul said, "Behold, I shew you a mystery; we shall not all sleep, but we shall all be changed, in a moment, in the twinkling of an eye, at the last trump: for the trumpet shall sound, and the dead shall be raised incorruptible, and we shall be changed" (see also Matt. 13:43; Phil. 3:21).

The second change was that "they received pure and shining garments." John recorded a change of raiment for the saints: "After this I beheld, and, lo, a great multitude, which no man could number, of all nations, and kindreds, and people, and tongues, stood . . . before the Lamb, clothed with white robes, and palms in their hands" (Rev. 7:9). The beautiful new clothing is symbolic of the finishing touches of perfection that God will make on the saints at the Second Coming (see also Zech. 3:2-4; Matt. 22:11; Rev. 3:5, 18; 7:13-15).

The third change was that "bright crowns were given them." Paul refers to the crown of the righteous: "Henceforth there is laid up for me a crown of righteousness, which the Lord, the righteous judge, shall give me at that day: and not to me only, but unto all them also that love his appearing" (2 Tim. 4:8). This third change can be viewed as symbolic of the crown of victory the saints will receive at the Second Coming (see also 1 Cor. 9:25; 1 Peter 5:4).

As the righteous are successfully undergoing their changes, the wicked reach the same spot. Seeing their own undone condition, they spontaneously cry for mercy and sink beneath the mount.

This scene portrays with considerable accuracy the early Advent movement. The message of Christ's soon coming gripped New England communities with biting intensity. People from all classes and cultures were motivated to respond to the call to prepare to go out to meet the Bridegroom. However, many were insincere or lacking in endurance. So when they experienced the mount of testing (not the least of which was the Great Disappointment), they, being unprepared, dropped out of sight. In short, by their own choosing they were not saved!

It should be noted, however, that this message was intended to motivate, rather than condemn, the people hearing it. It was not yet too late for them to heed its warning.

"The saints then passed on to a boundless plain, having the appearance like pure silver."[5] Now Foy's guide speaks for the first time, informing Foy that they had arrived at the place called the "plain of Paradise," in the vicinity of heaven. So vast was it that it seemed boundless. Filled with an effulgent glory, the plain took on the appearance of pure silver. The glory that Paul spoke about, "which shall be revealed in us," is soon to be shared with these saints. Foy goes on to say: "This heavenly host was then divided into flocks, some exceeding large in number, others but small. In the middle of each was an angel. These angels' garments were pure and white, and unto each of them was given a crown shining with great brightness. Their countenances were most lovely to behold; their wings like unto flaming fire."[6]

Before they enter the city, the saints are marshaled into various categories; some of the groups are large and others small. Certain angels, commanding in appearance and outstanding in beauty, are designated to take up position in the middle of each group. The guide explains that "these angels are they that have preached the gospel on the earth." Apparently, they had fulfilled certain vital roles in the promulgation of the gospel on the earth; thus their station among the redeemed.

In Foy's vision the watchcare of the angels is specifically highlighted. The truth of Hebrews 1:14, "Are they not all ministering spirits, sent forth to minister for them who shall be heirs of salvation?" not fully understood on earth, is revealed in heaven. Conscious appreciation is shown for the angels' labors.

Scene 3: *"I then beheld as it were a great gate before me. The gate was so tall, the height thereof I was unable to see. Before the gate stood a tall and mighty angel clothed in raiment pure and white; his eyes were like flaming fire, and he wore a crown upon his head, which lighted up this boundless plain. The angel raised his right hand and laid hold upon the gate, and opened it; and as it rolled upon its glittering hinges, he cried with a loud voice to the heavenly host, 'You're all welcome!' Then the guardian angels in the midst of the saints struck a song of triumph, and the saints,* *both small and great, sang with loud voices and passed within the gate; and the guardian angels arose upon their glittering wings and vanished from my sight. The inside of the gate appeared like glittering diamonds. Beneath our feet was as the appearance of pure glass.*"[7]

Foy's attention is now directed to the great gate before the city, a gate so tall that he wasn't able to see the top of it!

The centerpiece of the whole scene is not the gate, however. It is the tall and mighty angel standing before the gate. Foy finds his eyes riveted on this Personage, for He is the most striking of all. Who is He? He is none other than Jesus Christ, standing ready to welcome His followers into the city. Foy's description of Christ parallels that given by John, Daniel, and Ellen White in several respects. The chart on page 94 lists some of the similarities.

The majesty and supremacy of Christ is clearly evident in each of the accounts. In truth, human language is at best inadequate to describe the power and awesomeness of the scene.

Christ raises His hand, lays hold of the gate, and opens it. "As it rolled upon its glittering hinges, he cried with a loud voice to the heavenly host, 'You're all welcome!' "

The guardian angels in the midst of the saints strike a note of triumph, and the saints sing out with loud voices in response. The saints then pass within the gates and the angels fly away, vanishing from Foy's sight. He notes the awesome beauty of the city as he enters through the gates. The inside of the gate seems to be made of "glittering diamonds," and the ground has the "appearance of pure glass."

Scene 4: "*I then beheld countless millions of shining ones, coming with cards in their hands. These shining ones became our guides. The cards they bore shone above the brightness of the sun; and they placed them in our hands; but the names of them I could not read.*" [8]

Now Foy beholds a strange sight. Countless millions of "shining ones" approaching with "cards in their hands." The cards are a key part of the vision and are mentioned six times.

In *Early Writings* Ellen White also refers to cards being carried by angels in the heavenly city: "Then my attending angel directed me to the city again, where I saw four angels winging their way to the gate of the city. They were just presenting thegolden card to the angel at the gate." [9] "There is perfect order and harmony in the Holy City. All the angels that are commissioned to visit the earth hold a golden card, which they present to the angels at the gates of the city as they pass in and out." [10]

What is the card, and what does it represent? Neither William Foy nor Ellen White says specifically. However, after reading Foy's account, several points are clear: 1. The saints were given cards upon their arrival at the city. 2. The cards were glorious and of great value. Foy wasn't allowed to read the inscription on them. 3. Cards were given to the resurrected redeemed along with white raiment and crowns of brightness. 4. The redeemed in heaven were the bearers of cards.

The cards given to the righteous seem to be a form of identification and/or a means of conveying valuable information concerning the redeemed, information that only the redeemed are privy to. Later reference to cards in Foy's vision indicates that the information on the card was transferred to the forehead—or in more literal terms, impressed on the mind of the redeemed. This suggests references in Scripture that speak about the new name given to the righteous. One text says the new name was engraved on stone: "To him that overcometh will I give to eat of the hidden manna, and will give him a white stone, and in the stone a new name written, which no man knoweth saving he that receiveth it" (Rev. 2:17). According to another text, the name is written on the saints: "Him that

Prophetic Similarity Chart

	FOY *(Christian Experience)*	JOHN *(Revelation)*	DANIEL *(Daniel)*	WHITE *(Early Writings)*
Garments:	"clothed in raiment pure and white" (p. 10)	"clothed with a garment down to the foot" (1:13)	"clothed in linen" (10:5)	"clothed with a glorious white mantle from their shoulders to their feet" (p. 17)
Countenance:	"like the lightning" (p. 12)	"as it were the sun" (10:1)	"as the appearance of lightning" (10:6)	
Eyes:	"like flaming fire" (p. 10)	"as a flame of fire" (1:14)	"as lamps of fire" (10:6)	"as a flame of fire" (p. 16)
Legs, Feet:	"his legs were like pillars of flaming fire" (p. 12)	"his feet like unto fine brass, as if they burned in a furnace" (1:15)	"his feet like in colour to polished brass" (10:6)	"His feet had the appearance of fire" (p. 16)
Crown:	"he wore a crown upon his head" (p. 10)	"one sat like unto the Son of man, having on his head a golden crown" (14:14)		"upon His head were many crowns" (p. 16)
Arm, Hand:	"the angel raised his right hand, and laid hold upon the gate, and opened it; and . . . it rolled upon its glittering hinges" (p. 10)			"Jesus raised His mighty, glorious arm, laid hold of the pearly gate, swung it back on its glittering hinges" (p. 17)
Voice:	"he cried with a loud voice to the heavenly host, 'you're all welcome!'" (p. 10)			"and said to us, 'You have washed your robes in My blood, stood stiffly for My truth, enter in'" (p. 17)

overcometh will I make a pillar in the temple of my God, and he shall go no more out: and I will write upon him the name of my God, and the name of the city of my God, which is new Jerusalem, which cometh down out of heaven from my God: and I will write upon him my new name" (Rev. 3:12).

In light of the above comments, we would be safe in concluding that the card symbolizes the signature of Heaven on behalf of the bearer, a confirmation of divine acceptance. To the people in Foy's day, possession of this precious card must have been a strong incentive to press on to receive the eternal prize, to let nothing stand in the way.

After the angels had presented the cards to the redeemed, they took them by the hand and led them to a convocation of praise in a boundless place—a place with neither beginning nor end. No clouds or sky could be seen because of the countless millions of winged angels.

Then Foy speaks of two "innumerable multitudes." Those people in the first multitude are arrayed in white, "with cards upon their breasts." To each was given a "crown of brightness."

Interlude 1: *"The guide spoke, saying, 'These are they which have passed through death.'"* [11]

This first "innumerable multitude" is the resurrected redeemed!

Scene 5: *"There was arrayed before me in the spirit, an innumerable multitude which had not passed through death; their crowns were like the brightness of the stars; and in their right hands they held cards."* [12]

This is the second "innumerable multitude"—the translated redeemed. There is a strong parallel with this group and the 144,000 in Revelation 14. This multitude, Foy says, has the "brightness of the stars."

Scenes 6 and 7: *"I then saw an individual which had passed through death. Her brightness was beyond the expression of*

Believed to be a photo of Orrin,
William Foy's son (Michael W. Campbell)

A portrait of William Lawson, husband of
Nancy Foy Lawson, by William Matthew Prior
(Shelburne Museum)

A portrait of Nancy Foy Lawson, first cousin
of William Foy, by William Matthew Prior
(Shelburne Museum)

Silas Curtis, the minister who converted and
baptized William Foy in 1835 (White Estate)

The site of William Foy's second vision, the African Methodist Episcopal church on May Street on Beacon Hill, Boston (Boston Public Library)

The Second Methodist chapel on Bromfield Street in Boston, where Foy first shared his visions (Congressional Library Exhibits)

The African meetinghouse on Grove Street in Boston, the oldest standing Black church building in the United States and on the same street as Foy's house (Historic Buildings of Massachusetts)

Casco Street church in Portland, Maine, where Ellen White first heard William Miller in 1840 and most likely where William Foy also spoke (White Estate)

This piece appeared in the Portland *Tribune* on February 10, 1844, and was most likely referring to William Foy, who was lecturing in Portland, Maine, at the time. (White Estate)

WHEN WILL WONDERS CEASE? The *Millerites* of this city, have recently imported a great bull nigger, who has been rolling up the white of his eyes, showing his ivory, and astonishing the good people by his dreams and prognostications. It is said the fat and greasy black, can neither read nor write—but he told of the joys of the blest and the wailings of the damned with such a gusto, that even the weakest disciple of the prophet smacked his lips for more. What will be the end of these things, we cannot divine. As '43 has passed away and the signs that were to precede the burning of the world have in every instance failed, we do not wonder that the fanatics resort to some *new* measures to interest their disciples, and strengthen them in the faith. We soon expect to see this fat bull nigger, superbly dressed, seated in a chariot, and drawn through our streets, by the devoted disciples of Miller, who will bow down and worship him as a God.

NOTICE.

This is to notify the public that I shall not give a lecture at the Casco St. Meeting House, this afternoon, as was intended.

WILLIAM ELLIS FOY.

Portland, Feb. 27, 1844.

This cancellation notice appeared in the Portland *Advertiser* on February 27, 1844. (White Estate)

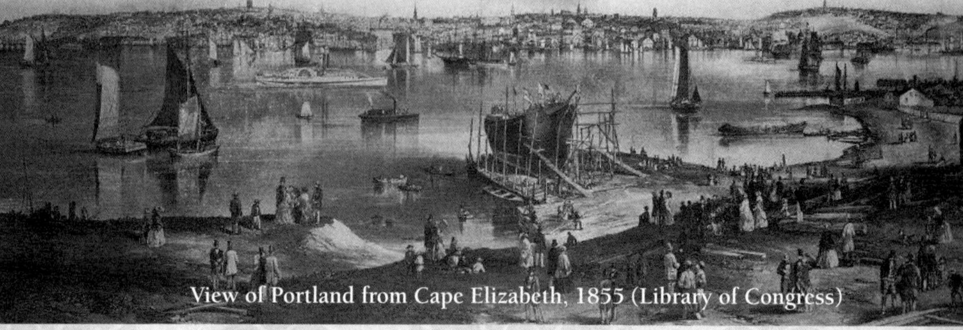

View of Portland from Cape Elizabeth, 1855 (Library of Congress)

Robert Harmon, Ellen White's father, who took her and the family to hear William Foy speak on numerous occasions (White Estate)

Earliest known image of Ellen G. White, taken in 1857 (White Estate)

Image of horse and sleigh in Portland in 1842 during the time the Harmons went to hear Foy by sleigh (Historic Portland)

Middle Street in Portland in 1844, location of building that housed Beethoven Hall

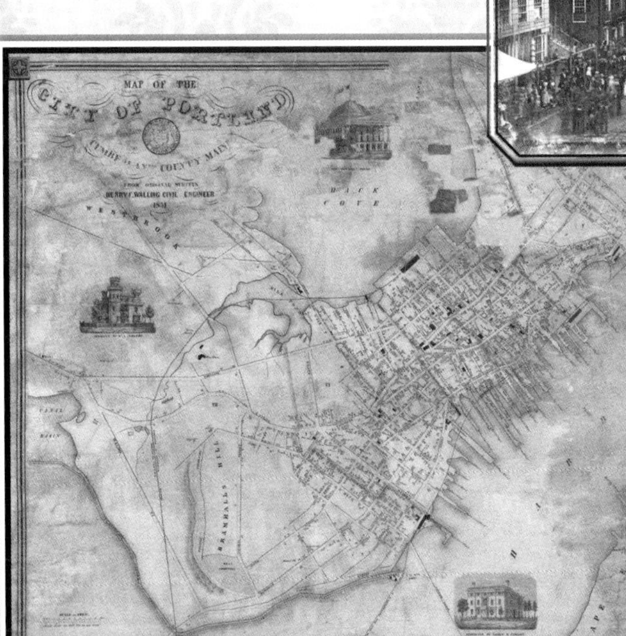

Map of Portland, Maine, 1851 (Library of Congress)

THE

CHRISTIAN EXPERIENCE

OF

WILLIAM E. FOY

TOGETHER WITH THE

TWO VISIONS

HE RECEIVED IN THE MONTHS OF JAN. AND FEB. 1842.

PORTLAND:
PUBLISHED BY J. AND C. H. PEARSON.
1845.

The cover and back of William Foy's 1845
booklet *Christian Experience* (James R. Nix)

24

TESTIMONIALS.

We, the undersigned, inhabitance of Boston, were witnesses of the apparently inanimate condition into which our brother, Wm. Ellis Foy, was thrown from some unknown cause, on the 18th of January 1842, when he laid two hours and a half; and again Febnary 4th, when he laid twelve hours and a half, during which, each time, he testifies that he experienced extraordinary visions of another world.

Charles Tash.	Francis Sanders.
George Williams.	John Thomas.
David Williams.	Andrew Lewis.
Edward Williams.	George Harris.

Dr. Henry Cummings, testifies: "I was present with our brother at the time of his visions. I examined him, but could not find any appearance of life, except around the heart."

Ann Foy testifies: "The first appearence of life I saw in him, was the raising of his right hand. He then arose upon his knees, and made signs for water, which was given him. He dipped his hand into it, and wet his forehead, and his speech immediately came to him. We then wished him to tell us, what things he had seen, and he answered, as soon as I receive strength, I will reveal unto you, that which the Lord has revealed unto me."

———

Copy of certificate of church membership.

This certifies that Bro. Wm. E. Foy, is a regular member, of the first Freewill Baptist Church, in Augusta, in good standing. And as such, we commend him to the fellowship of the people of God, of every name, whereever he may chance to meet them.

DANIEL PALMER,
Church Clerk.

Site of the former Beethoven Hall, Portland, Maine (Merlin D. Burt)

Sojourner Truth toured with Millerite circuits as a featured speaker and looked for the soon return of Christ. (Library of Congress)

William Still mentioned hearing William Miller preach in 1844 in his classic *The Underground Railroad* and believed the Advent to be the answer to the world's problems. (Library of Congress)

THE

LIFE, LABORS, AND TRAVELS

OF

ELDER CHARLES BOWLES,

OF THE FREE WILL BAPTIST DENOMINATION,

BY ELD. JOHN W. LEWIS.

TOGETHER WITH

AN ESSAY ON THE CHARACTER AND CONDITION OF THE AFRICAN RACE
BY THE SAME.

—ALSO,—

AN ESSAY ON THE FUGITIVE LAW

OF THE U. S. CONGRESS OF 1850,

BY REV. ARTHUR DEARING.

WATERTOWN:
INGALLS & STOWELL'S STEAM PRESS.
1852.

Frederick Douglass witnessed the stars fall in 1833 and confessed a longing for the return of Jesus. (Historical Society of Talbot County)

Charles Bowles was a believer in the second coming of Christ and possibly a Millerite. Featured is his biography by John Lewis. (University of North Carolina)

John Norton Loughborough (1832-1924) published the first history of Adventism and mentioned William Foy in both it and the revised second edition. (General Conference Archives)

Rise and Progress of the Seventh-day Adventists appeared in 1892, stating that William Foy initially obeyed the God-given command to share his visions, but "finally became exalted over the revelation, and thus lost his simplicity, hence the manifestation of this gift to him ceased, and soon after he sickened and died." (General Conference Archives)

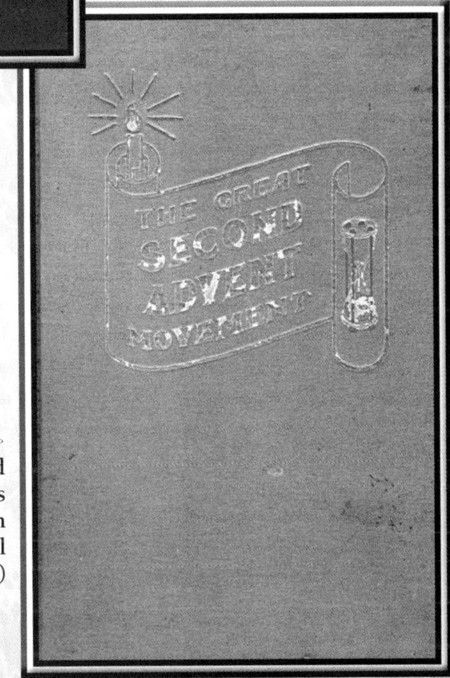

The Great Second Advent Movement, published in 1905, is the updated edition of *Rise and Progress* and features significantly more text on William Foy with greater accuracy. (General Conference Archives)

Ellen White speaking at Loma Linda in 1906, the year in which she remembered William Foy in an interview (White Estate)

Ellen White's interviewer, Dores E. Robinson, circa 1906, in White's office at Elmshaven (White Estate)

-5-

I had an interview with him. He wanted to see me, and I talked with him a little. They had appointed for me to speak that night, and I did not know that he was t ere. I did not know at first that he was there. While I was talking I heard a shout, and He is a great tall man, and the roof was rather low, and he jumped right up and down, and O he praised the Lord, praised the Lord, it was just what he had seen, just what he had seen. But they extolled him so I think it hurt him, and I do not know what became of him. His wife was so anxious. She sat looking at him, so that it distrubed him. "Now," said he, "you must not get where you can look at me when I am speaking. He had on an episcopalian robe. His wife sat by the side of me. She kept moveing about and putting her head behind me. What does she keep moving about so for? We found out when he came to his wife. "I did as you toàd me to," said she. "I hided myself, I did as you toôd me to." So that he should not see her face. She would be so anxious, repeating the words right after him with her lips. After the meeting was ended, and he came to look her up, she says to him, "I hided myself. You didn't see me." He was a very tall man, slightly colored. But it was remarkable testimonies that he bore.

I always sat right close by the stand. I know what I sat there fore now. It hurt me to breathe, and with the breaths xf all around me. I knew I could breathe easier right by the stand, so I always took my station.

Ques. Then you attended the lectures that Mr. Foy gave? He came to give it right to the hall, in the great hall where we attended, Beethoven Hall. That was quite a little time after the visions. It was in Portland, M aine. We went over to Cape Elizabeth to hear him lecture.

An original transcipt of the 1906 interview with Ellen White by Dores E. Robinson

Ellen White's bedroom in Elmshaven, where the 1906 interview was most likely conducted

The site of William Foy's house in East Sullivan, Maine (Merlin Burt)

Ruins of a well that Foy built on the property in East Sullivan, Maine (Merlin Burt)

Important Foy locations in East Sullivan, Maine (Merlin Burt)

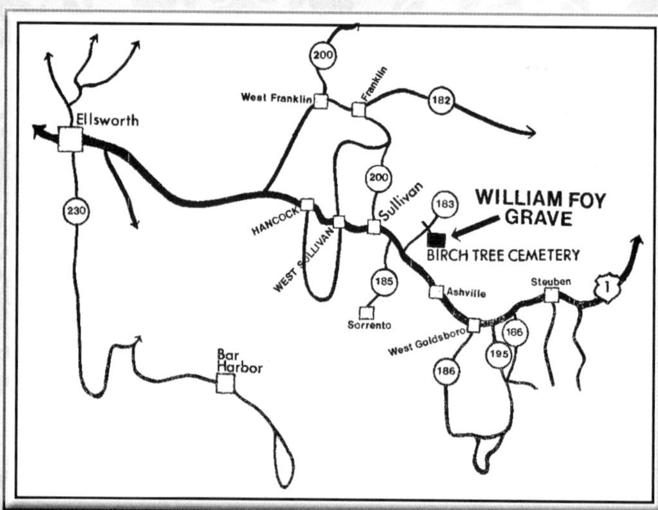

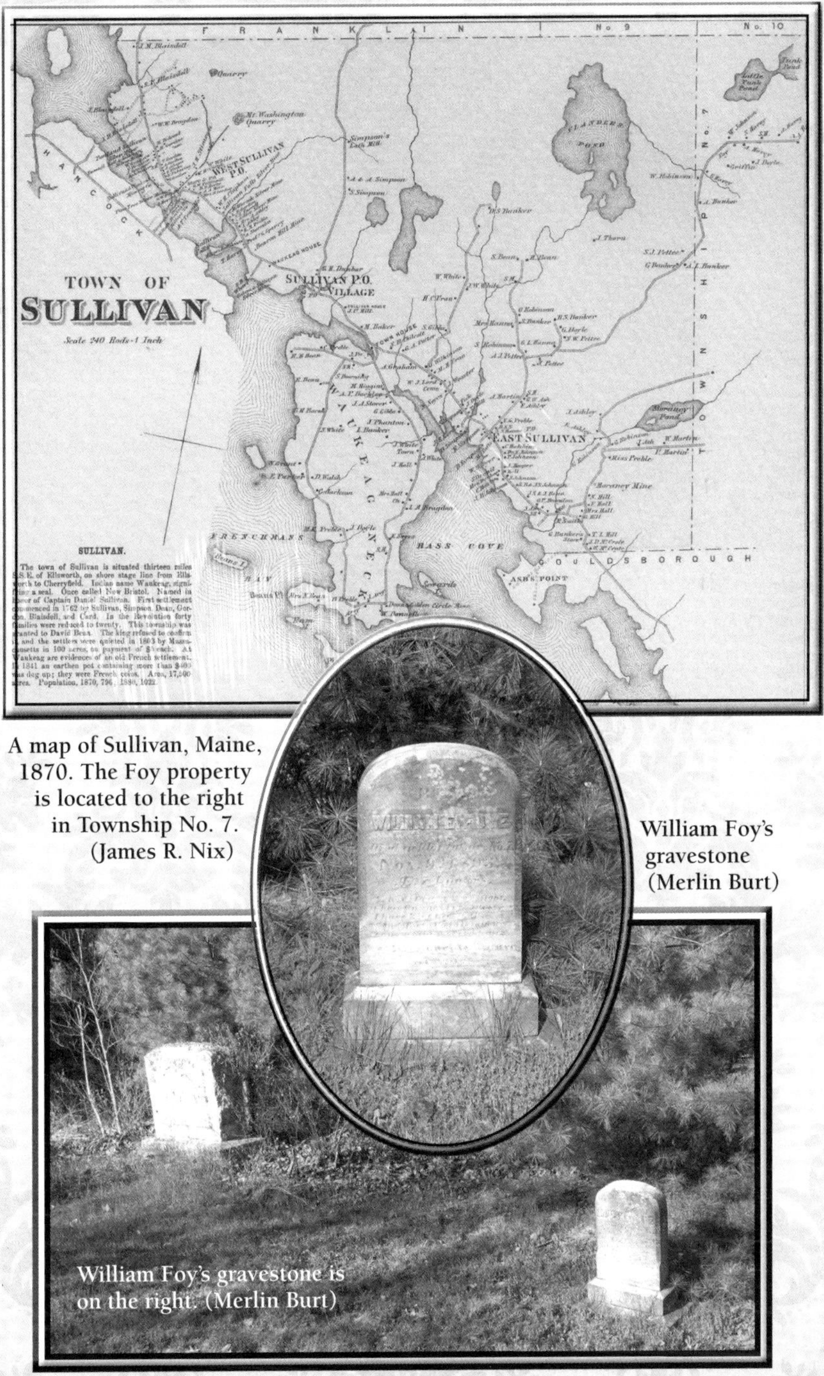

A map of Sullivan, Maine, 1870. The Foy property is located to the right in Township No. 7. (James R. Nix)

William Foy's gravestone (Merlin Burt)

William Foy's gravestone is on the right. (Merlin Burt)

Foy

RECORD OF A DEATH.

Name Wm. E. Foy
Place of Death No. 7 Pl.
Date of Death Nov 9 1893
Age, Years, 80 Months, Days
Place of Birth Augusta
Sex M Color B. Married, Single, Widowed, or Divorced.

Occupation Preacher
Cause of Death Chronic prostatitis and cystitis
Place of Burial E. Sullivan
Name of Father Unknown
Maiden Name of Mother "
Birthplace of Father "
Birthplace of Mother "
Occupation of Father "

Name and address of Physician (or other person) reporting said death.

Fred W. Bridgham, M.D.

STATE OF MAINE.

I hereby certify that the above death record is correct to the best of my knowledge and belief.

Clerk of

No 7 Pl.

Date OCT 27 1982

STATE REGISTRAR

Marian B. Perkins

A TRUE COPY ATTEST:

Void If Altered or Erased

William Foy's official record of death (White Estate)

mortals. . . . An angel then appeared flying through the midst of this boundless place." [13]

Momentarily Foy's attention is directed from the translated saints to an individual who had been resurrected. He comments that she was with her guardian angel and they made a stunning sight. As she passed him, she cried out with a lovely voice, "I am going to the gate to meet my friends."

An angel flew to one "which had not passed through death and cried with a loud voice saying, 'This is my mother!' He then became her guide." [14]

Heaven here seems excitingly real. There are real things to do, real places to go, real people to see. And the joy that is experienced will be inestimable. The whole scene vibrates with activity and motion. Everything is seasoned with joy, peace, and contentment. Everyone has his place, and everyone is satisfied.

Scene 8: *"I then beheld in the midst of this boundless place a high mountain like unto pure silver. It appeared perfectly round, and although I was unable to see through it, yet my vision extended around it. Around this mountain was a space in which stood no being. But after this vacant circle stood, as it appeared to be, a choir of angels, and as far as my sight could extend, throughout this boundless place stood the countless millions of the righteous. And, oh! The singing no mortal can describe!"* [15]

The focal point of the vision changes, not to a different location, but to a different scene. The resurrected and translated saints, along with the myriad of angels in the sky above, now face a "high mountain like unto pure silver," a mountain that "appeared perfectly round." Strangely, though Foy could not see through it, he could see around it.

There was a zone about the mountain that was completely empty—no being stood there. Beyond stood the redeemed; above circled the angels. There was indescribable singing going on, in a distinctive style. The angels would lead out in singing for a while, and then stop. The saints would catch the strain and repeat a chorus, only more loudly. This was done by first one group and then the other, until the entire plain echoed and reechoed with the praises.

We can safely conclude that this is none other than a grand heavenly worship ceremony of praise. The mount is the throne, or seat, of God, in the very heart of heaven. Certainly this seems similar to the "holy mountain of God" that Ezekiel spoke of, and the very spot that Satan desired, as recorded by Isaiah: "for thou hast said in thine heart, I will ascend into heaven, I will exalt my throne above the stars of God: I will sit also upon the mount of the congregation, in the sides of the north: I will ascend above the heights of the clouds; I will be like the most High" (Isa. 14:13, 14).

Continuing to describe the scene, Foy says:

"At the right side of the mountain appeared a mighty angel, with raiment like unto burnished gold, his legs were like pillars of flaming fire, his countenance was like the lightening, and his crown gave light to this boundless place, and those that had not passed through death could not look upon his countenance. I then beheld upon the side of this mount letters like pure gold, which said, 'THE FATHER AND THE SON.' Directly under these letters stood the mighty angel, whose crown lighted up the place, and all the heavenly host worshiped at his feet, round about the mountain." [16]

Surely, from the description given, the "mighty angel" is Christ Himself. His crown is so bright and powerful that it illuminated the entire plain. All of the host worship at His feet. Then Christ raises His right hand, which takes the appearance of a flaming sword. As He does so, all the translated saints are caught up to the top of the mountain. After heaven's books are checked, these saints are given cards with their name on them; it is at this point that the name on the card is "stamped," or settled, in the forehead, or mind. The investiture work is soon accomplished for the translated saints, and they are privileged to go to the top of the mount of God, where special deference is given to them.

Scene 9: *"We then stood again upon this pure sea of glass, before the mountain; and our bodies had become like transparent glass; but the being that was within the mountain, I was unable to behold."* [17]

The Being that Foy was unable to behold is none other than God the Father Himself. While the saints were drinking in the exquisite glories of the scene, a voice spoke from the mountain. As a result, all the multitude of saints and angels bowed at the feet of the "mighty angel" (Christ) and "worshiped Him" (see Phil. 2:9-11).

Scene 10: *"I then beheld this lower world, wrapt as it were in rolling mountains of flame."* [18]

Foy's attention changes abruptly from the scenes of glory to one that must have brought pangs of sadness to his heart. Turning from the sights of glory, he beholds the earth engulfed in "rolling mountains of flame." Young and old of a "countless multitude" cry for mercy. But there is stillness before the Lord. For these there can be no mercy, no reprieve.

Here then is the total extinction of the wicked and the eternal exaltation of the saints.

Interlude 2: *"I then began to converse with my guide, and inquired why there was no mercy for those whom I had seen in distress. He answered, 'The gospel has been preached unto them, and the servants have warned them, but they would not believe; and when the great day of God's wrath comes, there will be no mercy for them'"* [19]

Foy felt great concern for these hopeless ones. Why was there no mercy? The answer is a provocative warning to both the hearers of his day and ours. God's messengers had warned them, but they would not believe, the angel explains. Consequently, there can be no hope for them. Note how the angel changes his tenses. He says, "*When* the great day of God's wrath comes [showing there was still time], there *will* be no mercy for them."[20] In other words, there was still time, but time wouldn't last forever.

"*I then beheld in the middle of this boundless place a tree, the body of which was like unto transparent glass, and the limbs were like transparent gold, extending all over this boundless place. . . . This tree was also clothed in light proceeding from the mighty angel. Beneath this tree standing on the sea of glass were the countless millions of the righteous, arrayed in white raiment, with crowns on their heads, and cards upon their breasts; and in the multitude I saw some that I knew while they were living upon the earth, and they were all singing with loud voices and lifting up their glittering hands, plucking fruit from the tree; the fruit appeared like clusters of grapes in pictures of pure gold.*"[21]

The vision closes, not with the destruction of the wicked, but with the innumerable multitude, along with the angels, singing around the throne of God. Reference is made to a tree of light (see Rev. 2:7; 22:2, 14) standing on a sea of glass (see Rev. 4:6). Here at least seven rewards of the victorious are emphasized. The mercy of God is shown in the salvation and rescue of the righteous from death. The guidance of God is shown by the interest of the Godhead and heavenly intelligences. The joy of worship to God is demonstrated in the singing, praise, and adoration of the saints. The white raiment indicates purity from defilement and sin. The cards are symbolic of godly characters and the rights of the New Jerusalem. The tree of life and the sea of glass point to an eternal life without end.

Foy saw, in the redeemed multitude, some people that he knew on earth. He recounts seeing the luscious fruit on the tree of life and the great satisfaction of those who partook of it. The fruit, he adds, "appeared like clusters of grapes in pictures of pure gold."

Closing Scene: "*With a lovely voice, the guide then spoke to* *me and said, 'Those that eat of the fruit of this tree return to earth no more.' I raised my hand to partake of the heavenly fruit, that I might no more return to earth; but alas! I immediately found myself again in this lonely vale of tears."* [22]

Heaven had won his affection! Overwhelmed with the prospect of remaining in this heavenly land, Foy desired to eat of the heavenly fruit. But he was not now to remain. Immediately he found himself back on this dark earth.

We can see a number of ways in which this first vision compares with Revelation 14:

"144,000" Similarities

	FOY *(Christian Experience)*	JOHN *(Revelation 14)*
Translated Saints:	"multitude which had not passed through death" (p. 11)	"hundred and forty and four thousand, which were redeemed from the earth" (verse 3)
Companions With Jesus	"the mighty Angel then raised His right hand . . . , and . . . the multitude . . . were caught up to the top of the mountain" (p. 13)	"they . . . follow the Lamb whithersoever he goeth" (verse 4)
Holy Mount:	"were caught up to the top of the mountain [with Christ]" (p. 13)	"a Lamb stood on the mount Sion, and with him an hundred and forty and four thousand" (verse 1)
God's Name:	"their names came up out of the book in the form of cards, which were stamped upon their foreheads" (p. 13)	"having his Father's name written in their forehead" (verse 1)
God Speaks:	"a great voice spake in the mountain, and the place was mightily shaken" (p. 13)	"I heard a voice from heaven, as the voice of many waters, and . . . of a great thunder" (verse 2)
Sequential Connection:	"I then beheld this lower world, wrapt as it were in rolling mountains of flame, and in this fire, I saw a countless multitude crying for mercy" (p. 13)	"if any man worship the beast, and his image, and receive his mark in his forehead, or in his hand, the same shall drink of the wine of the wrath of God . . . he shall be tormented with fire and brimstone in the presence of the holy angels, and . . . of the Lamb" (verses 9, 11)
Saving Element:	"the gospel has been preached unto them . . . , but they would not believe; and when the great day of God's wrath comes, there will be no mercy for them" (p. 14)	"here is the patience of the saints: here are they that keep the commandments of God, and the faith of Jesus" (verse 12)

An understanding of Revelation 10 and 14 is vital to an understanding of the religious situation in America in the 1840s. One can't help noting the strong connecting lines between what Foy saw in his vision and the imagery of these two chapters. One gets the strong impression that God was seeking to convey a warning—not inconceivably, a warning concerning the Great Disappointment. Even though the overwhelming majority of Millerites were terribly shaken in that disappointment, the relating of Foy's visions must have accomplished much good to those sincere in heart who heard it.

NOTES

[1] Foy, *Christian Experience,* p. 9.
[2] *Ibid.*
[3] *Ibid.*
[4] *SDA Bible Dictionary,* p. 298.
[5] Foy, p. 9.
[6] *Ibid.,* p. 10.
[7] *Ibid.*
[8] *Ibid.,* pp. 10, 11.
[9] E. White, *Early Writings* (Washington, D.C.: Review and Herald Pub. Assn., 1945), p. 37.
[10] *Ibid.,* p. 39.
[11] Foy, p. 11.
[12] *Ibid.*
[13] *Ibid.*
[14] *Ibid.,* p. 12.
[15] *Ibid.*
[16] *Ibid.,* pp. 12, 13.
[17] *Ibid.*
[18] *Ibid.*
[19] *Ibid.,* p. 14.
[20] *Ibid.* (Italics supplied.)
[21] *Ibid.,* pp. 14, 15.
[22] *Ibid.,* p. 15.

Second Vision: Judgment

In as much as a little less than three weeks intervened between Foy's first and second visions, we will defer his reaction and that of his public until another chapter. Foy's second vision concerns the judgment, answering more fully the question that he asked about the wicked, "Why was there no mercy for those whom I had seen in distress?" His guide had responded that they were warned, "but they would not believe"; he left the discussion there.

This issue, which caused Foy such great concern, is fundamental to the gospel—namely, the fairness and equality of the judgment. Does God vindicate Himself while showing unfairness to the unsaved? What are the issues of the judgment? How will it be conducted?

We can be sure that God was seeking to direct man's attention to the subject of judgment at that time; the start of the investigative judgment (on October 22, 1844) was only about 20 months away. God has promised in His Word that He "will do nothing, but he revealeth his secret unto his servants the prophets" (Amos 3:7). In this vision to Foy, God was keeping His promise. He was letting man know beforehand that an event of great importance was imminent.

As in the first vision, no specific time span is given. A careful reading seems to indicate that this vision covered roughly the time from Foy's day to the occupancy of the New

*Grove Street was where Foy lived during the period he received visions.
Located on Beacon Hill, its crowded citizenry contained both Black and White
residents.*

Jerusalem. The primary difference in the two visions is one of
emphasis, not of time.

The first vision emphasized the reward and glory prepared
for the saints; the second vision focuses on the judgment and
requirements of the kingdom. One, in truth, complements the
other.

The major themes that stand out in the second vision are:
1. *Mercy and justice;* God is merciful, but each individual must
avail himself of that mercy when and how God's Word outlines.
2. *Fairness and impartiality;* God has no favorites. Every person,
old or young, Black or White, male or female, is judged on the
basis of his or her relationship to Christ and His Word. 3.
Compassion and delay; even though Christ could have come by

now, He has chosen to delay His coming to allow man to discern the times and take advantage of the available period of grace. 4. *Warnings and understanding;* God gives man warnings and indications of coming events because He wants him to be prepared. However, God is understanding and patient with man in his lack of perceptivity. 5. *Salvation and damnation;* even though God's grace, mercy, and compassion are extended to man, there comes a time when He must reward man according to his works, resulting in either eternal redemption or eternal destruction.

This vision also highlights the activity of angels on behalf of man. The work, the involvement, the love, and the interest of the angelic forces are interwoven throughout the vision narrative. Their role is not forced, but arises from their sincere interest in the welfare of man.

This second vision can be divided into eight different scenes that Foy witnessed, two interludes when his guide spoke, and a final closing scene.

"But the Lord in His mercy spared me to behold the evening of the fourth of February, 1842, when I met with the people of God in May Street." [1]

On a Friday, two and a half weeks after his first vision, Foy is presented with a second. It also takes place at a meeting with the people of God. Because of his deeply felt conviction that he must tell others of what he had seen in his first vision, and after trying unsuccessfully to write it out to his satisfaction, he is in church on Friday evening, experiencing a major spiritual battle. Though the church was engaged in exhortation and prayer, he experienced none of what he referred to as the "sensible presence of God."

The church became crowded, and he gave his seat to one of his friends who had been standing all evening. While he himself was standing, Foy suddenly heard "a voice, as it were, in the spirit, speaking unto me." He fell to the floor and "knew nothing about this body, until 12 hours and a half had passed away."

Scene 1: *"It appeared to me that I was a spirit separate from this body, standing upon the earth alone. No other being appeared to be with me."* [2]

To be on the earth alone must have been a tremendously moving experience. Possibly this solitude infers that everyone must appear at the judgment bar individually.

The earth appeared perfectly level. Foy discovers that he can look far and deep in any direction, without any obstruction to his view.

Scene 2: *"I then beheld a cloud gently rising out of the west, which came up and covered the sun so that it was darkened."* [3]

Mystified, Foy beholds a cloud rising with ethereal effect from the west. It totally covers the sun, so that it is now as dark as it once was light (see Amos 8:9). We have good reason to conclude that "from the west" symbolizes the "sunset" or ending of time.

Into the midst of this unnatural darkness "something beyond the expression of mortal man burst forth from the heavens, from the south even unto the north." Foy says it was like "a flaming bar of fire." [4]

What had he seen? Foy had just seen heaven's judgment tribunal set up, with the Divine Judge in attendance. This unquestionably is one of the most awesome and solemn scenes that human eyes can rest upon (see Dan. 7:9-14; Eze. 22:20-22; Ps. 97:2-4).

Scene 3: *"I then beheld innumerable multitudes coming from the four quarters of the earth, and were assembled before this bar, and there stood in solemn silence."* [5]

Foy watches fascinated as the first of four multitudes approaches the bar. The first multitude is made up of two parts—the righteous and the wicked. Apparently these people are alive at the time of Christ's return. They assemble before the bar, standing in "solemn silence" (see 2 Cor. 5:10; Acts 17:31; Rom. 14:12; 2:16; Rev. 20:12; Matt. 25:32). Each individual seems visibly shaken as the process begins. Some are saved and some aren't, despite God's express desire to save all mankind.

RIGHTEOUS LIVING TRANSLATED	WICKED LIVING DESTROYED
"bodies of the saints were changed"	"unable to pass [the bar]"
"becoming like transparent gold"	"world beneath appeared to be wrapt in darkness and fire"
"clothed in light and shining garments"	"sunk from my sight, crying for mercy"
"crowns of brightness were placed up on their heads"	
"shining cards upon their breasts"	
"singing sweetly, they passed through the bar of fire"	

The separation is severe and heartrending. Often children are changed and pass safely through the bar while "unholy mothers . . . sink below."

Scene 4: *"I then beheld an innumerable multitude coming up from the waters, and an innumerable multitude coming up out of the earth."* [6]

Here are the second and third multitudes Foy sees. Apparently they are the righteous dead; they go directly through the bar.

Scene 5: *"I then beheld a multitude coming up out of the earth, and some of them I knew whose names were enrolled in the church books on earth."* [7]

Evidently this fourth multitude is smaller, because Foy does not describe the group as being innumerable. He actually recognizes some whose names are enrolled in church books — who only profess to be members of the body of Christ. Among them are educators, church administrators — and even clergymen!

These are earth's best! Yet in spite of their high callings, they are not found worthy. Sadly, they too cry for mercy and sink along with the worst of sinners. As Jesus said: "Not every one that saith unto me, Lord, Lord, shall enter into the kingdom of heaven" (Matt. 7:21).

The lesson here is universally relevant. Neither profession nor politics saves a person; only a relationship with Christ is valid. In spite of their professions and morals, when they do not pass the bar they are grouped with the worst of sinners (see Matt. 7:21-23).

Scene 6: *"As we passed the bar, we entered upon a boundless place which was lighted up with great brightness. Near the place through which we passed, I beheld a mighty angel clothed in pure white raiment, having a crown of brightness on his head. He appeared to be gazing through the bar, and his eyes, like lamps of fire, were fixed with steadfastness upon the earth. He stood with his right foot placed before him, as though walking; and his object appeared to be to reach the earth. But three steps remained for him to take. Against his breast and across his left hand was, as it were, a trumpet of pure silver; and a great and terrible voice came from the midst of the boundless place, saying, 'The sixth angel hath not yet done sounding.'"* [8]

This is an entirely new scene. Foy and the other righteous have passed the bar, and now they enter a "boundless place"— Paradise, a great expanse illuminated with a "great brightness" from the "mighty angel."

This angel is vitally important because, looking back from our vantage point, we recognize that he was the one who held the key to an understanding of the judgment-hour message; he also held the light that might have enabled the people to avoid the Great Disappointment.

Foy sees this angel poised, ready to go on an important mission. His destination is the earth, and he has a particular function to fulfill there. He has only three more steps to go when a voice calls out, halting him.

A comparison of the mighty angel that Foy saw with the mighty angel that John beheld in Revelation 10 shows distinct parallels and helps to establish the identity of this angel:

The Parallel: Both the "mighty angel" of Foy's vision and the one in Revelation 10:1 represent Jesus Christ.

1. The description of both angels is the same.

2. The time sequence of both complement each other.

The Point: There were yet unfulfilled events before the Second Coming.

1. The angel was held up from reaching the earth because the sixth angel was not finished with his work (Rev. 9:13-21).

2. Revelation 10, of which this angel is the central figure, stands as a parenthesis between the sixth and seventh angels. The chapter opens with the descent and description of this "mighty angel."

3. The "mighty angel" illustrated the reality of unfulfilled prophecy.

4. The events of the seventh angel would transpire just before the second coming of Christ, which showed there had to be yet more time.

The Possibility: The Great Disappointment could have been avoided.

1. If this scene had sparked deeper study of Revelation 10 and 11, at least some of the people could have been sufficiently fortified to avoid the Great Disappointment.

2. An understanding of the meaning of the "little book" in Revelation 10 and the need to "prophesy again" would have given immediate guidance, even after the Great Disappointment.

3. The three steps here, and later the three platforms, could have led to further study of Revelation 14:6-12 and the part that had yet to be fulfilled, namely, the third angel's message.

At best, we can now only reflect on the possibilities. Yet we can see graphically how God sought to protect His people against the Disappointment by sending a message that pointed to the Bible and the needed light. Recognizing this, we can be encouraged as we face the problems of our day.

The activity in this heavenly place is rich in detail and imagery. Foy's attention is caught by the beauty and grandeur of myriads of angels. Overwhelmed, he says, "I beheld countless millions of bright chariots." He describes the chariots as being perfectly square and having the appearance of pure gold. According to Psalm 68:17, the chariots of God are the angels who do His bidding (see also Isa. 66:15; Hab. 3:8). Once again we note the close cooperation of angels in the affairs of man. This wonderful organization of heaven is an enduring comfort.

As Foy watches this breathtaking sight, another scene begins to command his interest. In response to some directive, one of the chariots "arose upon its wings of fire, and an angel followed after the chariot; and the wings of the chariot and the wings of the angel cried as with one loud voice, saying, 'Holy! Holy!'"

After having seen all the multitudes appear before the bar, some to pass, some to sink, Foy sees another person allowed entrance into the "boundless place." The chariot goes to a mountain and picks up an inhabitant from the earth, who also was arrayed in white raiment and given a "crown of brightness." "He stepped into the chariot with the angel, and in a moment he was in this boundless place."[9]

At this point Foy appears to grow ecstatic. He recognizes the person from earth. He identifies him as Elder George Black, the pastor of the congregation at Southack Street, where he had his first vision. Two weeks after this second vision, George Black died.

A similar occurrence took place in Ellen White's experience. In her vision of heaven, she saw two Millerite preachers whom she knew. After describing some of the glories of the New Jerusalem, she records in *Early Writings:* "We all went under the tree and sat down to look at the glory of the place, when Brethren Fitch and Stockman, who had preached the gospel of the kingdom, and whom God had laid in the grave to save them, came up to us and asked us what we had passed through while they were sleeping."[10]

Thus George Black, a Baptist minister; Charles Fitch, a Presbyterian minister; and Levi Stockman, a Methodist minister—all of whom died in the hope of Christ's soon coming—stand with the saved. Men of different races and religions—Black and White, Presbyterian, Baptist, and Methodist—all together in heaven!

Scene 7: *"I then saw in the midst of the place an innumerable multitude, arrayed in white raiment, standing in a perfect square."*[11]

Foy is shown other sights that must have brought cheer to the hearts of his hearers. He describes yet another multitude, this one having five characteristics: (1) they were "arrayed in white raiment"; (2) they were "standing in a perfect square"; (3) they were wearing "crowns of unfading glory upon their heads"; (4) they were "the size of children 10 years of age"; and (5) they sung "a song which the saints and angels could not sing."

In light of the knowledge that infants are allowed to pass the bar, even without their parents if necessary, it is conceivable that heaven will be populated with children as well as adults. We are reminded of Zechariah's words: "And the streets of the city shall be full of boys and girls playing in the streets thereof" (Zech. 8:5).

One of the most refreshing characteristics of Foy's vision is that many different people are included in the heavenly picture. Details in his account portray a variety of life's categories—men, women, Blacks, Whites, children, mothers, infants, rich, and poor.

Foy goes on to describe the river of life, and witnesses angels drinking from it with "cups like pure gold."

Scene 8: *"Then came one unto me clothed in white, whom I call my guide—he led me to a place like unto a narrow door."* [12]

This is the first time Foy's guide appears in this vision. Now has come the time for an explanation of judgment. Foy has already witnessed the judgment scene, and now in something like a flashback his guide reveals to him certain details of the judgment.

Through a narrow door, Foy beholds a mighty angel with two books open before him: one on the right hand and the other on the left. Foy is impressed with how carefully the angels preserve the records upon which the decisions of judgment are based.

Interlude 1: *"My guide then spake to me, saying, 'They that repent of their sins on the earth are blotted out of the book on the left and recorded on the right.'"* [13]

The recording system is simple yet efficient.

Foy becomes aware of "angels ascending and descending to and from the earth." Like Jacob of old, he is allowed a view of the close contact between heaven and earth: Jacob "dreamed, and behold a ladder set up on the earth, and the top of it reached to heaven: and behold the angels of God ascending and descending on it" (Gen. 28:12). The angels Foy saw gave reports to the recording angels, who faithfully and accurately recorded the information.

Interlude 2: *"My guide now informed me what I must do."* [14]

Foy has been privileged to see things that mortal eyes have never beheld in reality. He has been shown what is to come—the glory and the despair, the joy and the gloom, the exhilaration and the forlornness. And he has felt the emotions of men and women confronted with the judgment.

Now his guide informs him of what he must do. He outlines a twofold commission: "Thy spirit must return to yonder world, and thou must reveal those things which thou hast seen." It isn't Foy's time to remain in glory; rather, he must return to earth. He has a job to do, a responsibility to carry, a task to accomplish. All the marvelous things he has seen—the glories, triumphs, joys, rewards, and bounties—must be shared with others. But not these alone. The judgment—its destruction, calamity, solemnness, and inevitableness—must also be shared. To everyone, everywhere, Foy is to be God's mouthpiece. He has been an eyewitness, he has actually experienced what he is now commanded to relate.

"Warn thy fellow creatures to flee from the wrath to come." With these words borrowed from John the Baptist, the guide gives Foy the second part of his commission. Foy has been affected in a vicarious yet personal way. He has seen multitudes sink beneath the bar into destruction. Church members, teachers, preachers, community leaders, mothers and fathers and children—all missing out on heaven and experiencing eternal destruction. Having seen the unutterable joys of heaven weighed against the heinousness of separation from God, Foy is to become a signalman, he is to sound the alarm of coming calamity and lift hearts by speaking of Jesus. His source of strength is summed up in the words of David, "Blessed are all they that put their trust in him" (Ps. 2:12), and his authority in the words of John, "He that believeth on the Son hath everlasting life: and he that believeth not the Son shall not see life; but the wrath of God abideth on him" (John 3:36).

"How can I return to yonder world?" Foy responds.

"I will go with thee, and support and help thee, to declare these things unto the world," affirms his guide.

The constant support and help of the guide is all the assurance that Foy needs. "I will go" is his response as he commits himself to the fulfilling of the commission given him.

Closing Scene: *"I then beheld this lower world. It seemed as though the veil which had separated it from the boundless place in which I stood was removed."* [15]

Perhaps this final scene was given to deepen the impression of the close interaction between heaven and earth. Foy is exhilarated and comforted by seeing, as it were, a veil removed from between heaven and earth: "They had both become as one." He sees that "the saints and angels were passing continually to and from the earth."

The earth appears in its restored state, "like a calm sea of transparent gold; above, no cloud or sky appeared, but the air was perfectly pure, and of a silvery brightness." Again he hears the melodious singing of "saints and angels in heaven and on the earth."

While that overwhelming scene of consummate loveliness was lingering on Foy's mind, his guide "then spread his wings, and brought my spirit gently to the earth, then soared away; and immediately I found myself in the body." [16]

This vision is pregnant with meaning and inspiration for the child of God in any age. The scenes described, the truths imparted, the admonitions conveyed—all bear the divine imprint. But most important, the vision encourages each of us to prepare for an event that is yet future—the final judgment day for the universe.

NOTES

[1] Foy, *Christian Experience*, p. 16.
[2] *Ibid.*, p. 16.
[3] *Ibid.*
[4] *Ibid.*
[5] *Ibid.*
[6] *Ibid.*, p. 17.
[7] *Ibid.*
[8] *Ibid.*, p. 18.
[9] *Ibid.*, p. 19.
[10] Ellen White, *Early Writings*, p. 17.
[11] Foy, p. 19.
[12] *Ibid.*, pp. 19, 20.
[13] *Ibid.*, p. 20.
[14] *Ibid.*
[15] *Ibid.*
[16] *Ibid.*, p. 21.

Third Vision: Providence

Foy's third vision has a different thrust from the first two: it is concerned primarily with the theme of the gospel on earth and with providential guidance, while the prior visions have involved celestial and apocalyptic scenes, most of them taking place in heaven.

Foy's visions follow a logical order. They seem to follow a type of deductive progression; that is, they proceed from the general and broad to the specific and detailed. The first vision dealt with the sweeping theme of the final triumph of the faithful, along with the theme of judgment. The second vision dealt primarily with the judgment and preparedness, along with the theme of final victory. The subject matter of the third vision precedes the judgment—it emphasizes events on earth prior to the Second Coming.

Unfortunately, we are dependent on secondary sources for the details of this third vision. John Loughborough, an early pioneer of the Seventh-day Adventist Church and author of the two earliest denominational history books, makes reference to Foy's ministry and he gives us a synopsis of his third vision.[1]

The themes of this vision may be outlined as follows: 1. *Guiding providence;* God leads His people from one point of truth to another, until finally they are brought into the kingdom. 2. *Tenacious commitment;* the true believers remain firm when others drop out. 3. *Testing truth;* three platforms, or steps, sift the elements of truth. God's truth effectively becomes a judging agent here on earth. 4. *Final triumph;* the ultimate arrival of the saints at the Holy City is a result of their fidelity to truth.

We do not know where Foy was when he had this vision, whether in Boston or any of the other places he visited in his ministry. Apparently the vision took place prior to October 22, 1844 (the day of the Great Disappointment), perhaps during the middle part of 1844. The vision can be divided into four scenes, as described by Loughborough:

Scene 1: "In this [third vision] he was shown the pathway of the people of God through to the heavenly city."[2]

Scene 2: "He saw a great platform, or step, on which multitudes of people gathered. Occasionally, one would drop through this platform out of sight, and of such a one it was said to him, 'Apostatized.'"[3]

In another account, Loughborough quotes Foy as describing the steps as "steps of fire."[4]

Scene 3: "Then he saw the people rise to a second step, or platform, and some there also dropped through the platform out of sight."[5]

Scene 4: "Finally a third platform appeared, which extended to the gates of the Holy City. A great company gathered with those who had advanced to this platform."[6]

According to Loughborough, Foy did not understand the third vision. The pathway would be easy enough to understand, and the eventual destination, the heavenly city. But what was intended by the three steps? Foy did not have an explanation.

Interestingly, in two separate visions, Ellen White viewed scenes very similar to those described by Foy. In her account of her first vision, received only a few months after Foy had received his visions, Ellen penned these words: "While I was praying at the family altar, the Holy Ghost fell upon me, and I seemed to be rising higher and higher, far above the dark world. I turned to look for the Advent people in the world, but could not find them, when a voice said to me, 'Look again, and look a little higher.' At this I raised my eyes, and saw a straight and narrow path, cast up high above the world. On this path the Advent people were traveling to the city, which was at the farther end of the path. They had a bright light set up behind them at the beginning of the path, which an angel told me was the midnight cry. This light shone all along the path and gave light for their feet so that they might not stumble. If they kept their eyes fixed on Jesus, who was just before them, leading them to the city, they were safe."[7]

More than 10 years later Ellen White published the account of another vision, which began with these words: "I saw a company who stood well guarded and firm, giving no countenance to those who would unsettle the established faith of the body. God looked upon them with approbation. I was shown three steps—the first, second, and third angels' messages."[8]

Thus Mrs. White's vision explains Foy's: the steps, or platforms, represent the messages of the three angels, recorded in Revelation 14:6-12. The platforms were called "steps of fire" possibly in reference to the bright beginnings of the Advent movement.

The first angel's message as stated in Revelation 14:6, 7, says: "And I saw another angel fly in the midst of heaven, having the everlasting gospel to preach unto them that dwell on the earth, and to every nation, and kindred, and tongue, and people, saying with a loud voice, Fear God, and give glory to him; for the hour of his judgment is come: and worship him that made heaven, and earth, and the sea, and the fountains of waters."

To the Millerites, the message referred to the time when God would come and judge the world at the Second Coming. It became their watchword. Their cry was "The angel of God declares it: the judgment is come!" The hearts of men, women, boys, and girls were seized. Everywhere was proclaimed the judgment-hour message!

Unfortunately, that is all they saw. The brightness and glory of the first angel so filled their eyes that they but faintly perceived the second angel, and the third not at all.

As people gathered on the platform of the first angel's message, they embraced it with a fervency that this world has seldom seen. Yet some, having embraced the message, defected, or fell off. This was reflected in Ellen White's first vision, as well.

Ellen White (November 26, 1827 - July 16, 1915) was signally used by God in the founding and building of the Seventh-day Adventist Church. The photo was taken in 1877.

The message of the first angel settled in and grew to become a worldwide force. Arthur Spalding, church historian, eloquently comments on the progressive revelation of truth during this period: "The truth of God is ever unfolding, ever revealing new facets, new depths; and the education of those who follow that truth is progressive. The three angels' messages are no exception to this universal rule in the revelations of God. Since the days of our pioneers, who at first perceived only the girders of this body of truth, the meaning and the spiritual content of the three angels' messages have been made more and more apparent; and the end of their wealth of knowledge and inspiration has not yet been reached."[9]

After the Great Disappointment, the judgment-hour message was interpreted as referring to the investigative judgment, which began in heaven on October 22, 1844 (see Dan. 7-9). The records of men from the beginning of time would be examined; through judgment of their lives, the heavenly sanctuary would be vindicated.

The first angel's message wasn't to end with the proclamation of the judgment hour. It was to continue as a bulwark against evolution, atheism, and the fallacies of science that honor man instead of God. It focuses our attention on the ministration of Christ on our behalf in the Most Holy Place, and by identifying God as the true Creator, it calls attention to the Sabbath of the Fourth Commandment.

The second angel gave the warning "Babylon is fallen, is fallen, that great city, because she made all nations drink of the wine of the wrath of her fornication" (Rev. 14:8). Babylon was interpreted as those Christian churches that, mixing doctrinal error with truth, virtually apostatized from the apostolic foundations.

During 1844, especially during the summer, there was a general separation of the Advent believers from the mainline churches, who in turn closed their doors to them. By October these Adventists were so thoroughly estranged that except they should repudiate their Advent experience, there would be no returning to their former churches.

The disappointment that ensued when Christ didn't come on October 22, 1844, essentially ended the Millerite movement. Following this disappointment, many not only gave up their faith in the Advent teaching but totally repudiated Christ.

The third platform that Foy envisioned extended to the city of God, and the people of God proceeded on it with joy. This is the final platform; by mounting each platform in turn, the pathway to the city is reached.

When correlated with the three angels' messages, we must conclude that this third platform represents the third angel's message of Revelation 14:9-12: "And the third angel followed them, saying with a loud voice, If any man worship the beast and his image, and receive his mark in his forehead, or in his hand, the same shall drink of the wine of the wrath of God, which is poured out without mixture into the cup of his indignation; and he shall be tormented with fire and brimstone in the presence of the holy angels, and in the presence of the Lamb: and the smoke of their torment ascendeth up for ever and ever: and they have no rest day nor night, who worship the beast and his image, and whosoever receiveth the mark of his name. Here is the patience of the saints: here are they that keep the commandments of God, and the faith of Jesus."

The first and second angels' messages were proclaimed to some extent by the Millerites, but they never really came to grips with the message of the third angel. Consequently, it was not until May 1847, two and a half years after the Great Disappointment, that anything was published on the third angel's message. In the pamphlet *A Word to the "Little Flock,"* James and Ellen White and Joseph Bates combined their efforts to put their newly studied views into print.

In this pamphlet, in an article by James White entitled "Thoughts on Revelation 14," we find the first published reference to the third angel's message. White states: "All classes of second advent believers agree that the angel brought to view in the sixth and seventh verses of this chapter represents the advent message to the church and world. . . . The third angel's message was, and still is, a WARNING to the saints. . . . It is plain that we live in the time of the third angel's message."

Since that time, the phrase *third angel's message* has been an idiom of Sabbathkeeping Adventists that succinctly sums up the thrust of the movement. We might therefore say that this new Advent group stood on Foy's third platform.

Foy's vision of the platforms stresses that the angelic messages are progressive. They do not exist separately and autonomously. Each depends on the others; all three are needed to lift believers to the heavenly pathway and thence to the Holy City.

Along with the other visions, this one shows us the ever-unfolding nature of truth. It is both a comfort and a warning.

NOTES

[1] Loughborogh, *The Great Second Advent Movement,* pp. 146, 147.

[2] *Ibid.,* p. 146.

[3] *Ibid.*

[4] J. N. Loughborough, *Rise and Progress of the Seventh-day Adventists* (Battle Creek, Mich.: General Conference of Seventh-day Adventists, 1892), p. 71.

[5] Loughborough, *The Great Second Advent Movement, p. 146.*

[6] *Ibid.*

[7] Ellen White, *Early Writings,* p.14.

[8] *Ibid.,* p.258

[9] Arthur Spalding, *Orgin and History of the Seventh-day Adventists* (Washington, D.C.: Review and Herald Pub. Assn., 1961), vol. 1, p. 182.

Following the Great Disappointment Ellen White received various visions showing God's providence ever leading His people upward.

CHAPTER 13

Fourth Vision: Unknown

In a 1906 interview with D. E. Robinson, Ellen White spoke of Foy, his visions, and his experiences. She states that Foy had four visions. She was definite, even adamant, concerning it: "Then another time, there was Foy that had . . . visions. He had . . . four visions. . . . He had all these before I had them. They were written out and published, and it is queer that I cannot find them in any of my books. But we have moved so many times. He had four." [1]

Without specific information on this fourth vision, we can only attempt to piece together the circumstances and suggest some possibilities. Ellen White states that they were written out and published, and she indicates that at one time she possessed a copy of them.

We might ask, Where did Foy have this vision? Possibly it took place in Portland, Maine, a few months before the Great Disappointment. Ellen White said that she heard him lecture there, at Beethoven Hall: "We went over to Cape Elizabeth to hear him lecture. Father always took me with him when we went, and he would be going in a sleigh, and he would invite me to get in, and I would ride with them. That was before I got any way acquainted with him." [2]

Reviewing one of the meetings that she attended, she described an incident that seemed to involve Foy: "He was in a large congregation, very large. He fell right to the floor. I do not know what they were doing in there, whether they were listening to preaching or not. But at any rate he fell to the floor. I do not know how long [it] was, about three quarters of an hour, I think, and he had all these before I had them."[3]

Possibly this experience was Foy having his fourth vision. Whether it comprised other scenes concerning pre- or post-Advent events, or whether it contained information concerning this future role, the Advent movement, or the Second Coming, there is no way of knowing.

We do know that Foy had all of his visions before Ellen White had her first. The latter states that she heard Foy lecture "quite a little time after the visions [Foy's]." And she pays Foy's prophetic ministry a signal compliment: "It was remarkable testimonies that he bore."

NOTES

[1] Ellen White, "William Foy," Document File 231.
[2] *Ibid.*
[3] *Ibid.*

A Duty to Warn

William Foy's commission and his response have to be examined in light of the great issues of the day—slavery, racial prejudice, and theological differences. His decision to accept and work to fulfill his commission was not made without a struggle.

Following his first vision—concerning the ultimate victory of the saints—Foy felt the burden to immediately relate to others the things he had seen, although he had not been specifically told to do so.

"The duty to declare the things which had thus been shown to me, to my fellow creatures, and warn them to flee from the wrath to come, rested with great weight upon my mind." [1]

The sights and sounds he had experienced were awe-inspiring, but he knew that God hadn't made him privy to these things simply for his own entertainment. To Foy, as to Jeremiah of old, "his word was in mine heart as a burning fire shut up in my bones, and I was weary with forbearing, and I could not stay" (Jer. 20:9).

Foy goes on to say:

"But I was disobedient, settling upon this point for an excuse, that my guide did not command me so to do; and I thereby brought darkness and death upon my soul. But I could find no peace or comfort. I began to doubt whether indeed my soul had ever been converted." [2]

Foy realized that he was wrong for not immediately sharing with others what he had seen. Darkness and gloom rested on him. He could not find peace or comfort. With the weight so heavy and the guilt so strong, he reflected again on what was the center and joy of his life—his experience with Christ.

Seeking to sublimate his guilt, he met often with the people of God, but with no relief. That stands to reason. Peace and comfort come not from meeting with the people of God, but in responding to the God of the people.

In the depths of frustration and despair, he said, "I could get no access in prayer." Obviously there was no alternative. He must go! He must tell! He must reveal! He must warn!

"But the Lord in his mercy spared me to behold the evening of the fourth of February 1842, when I met with the people of God in May Street." [3]

It was there that, depressed, despondent, and disobedient, Foy was taken into vision for the second time—confirming that he was yet acceptable to God.

In his second vision, which dealt with the judgment, Foy was again forcefully impressed with the awesome events coming on the world and the need for everyone to prepare for them. But in this vision his guide specifically informed him of what he must do. He must return to the world and reveal the things that he saw; he must warn the people. There was now no mistaking his charge, no excuse for disobedience. To turn down this charge would have exceeded disobedience; it would have been rebellion.

It was late Friday evening when he entered into this second vision. It lasted 12½ hours, so he came out of it on Saturday morning. A group of people had stayed with him, and when he came out of vision, according to Ann Foy, they "then wished him to tell us what things he had seen, and he answered, 'As soon as I receive strength, I will reveal unto you that which the Lord has revealed unto me.'" [4]

Though having agreed to fulfill his task, he yet faced a spiritual dilemma. "Notwithstanding the command of my guide, and my solemn promise to declare these things to the world, I was at first exceedingly unwilling so to do, and it was three days before I revealed them in public manner." Foy continued to battle some difficult issues. "The message was so different—and the manner in which the command was given, so different from any I had ever heard of, and knowing the prejudice among the people against those of my color, it became very crossing."[5]

The message was unquestionably different. The judgment theme; the knowledge that some outstanding church leaders

Around 1844 the derision against Miller and the Advent believers increased. This poster against Millerites, published in the 1840s, conspicuously shows Blacks connected with the movement.

and members were unprepared; the reward of the righteous; the destruction of the wicked; the delay emphasis in the visions, especially that which is implied when referring to the sixth angel—all these elements combined to make the message radically different. But perhaps the most unusual aspect was the manner by which he had received the message—by vision! Even in those days, a person who tried to communicate visionary messages met, for the most part, with outright skepticism or leery caution.

For two days these feelings of apprehension rested heavily on his mind. The breakthrough came when in an experience similar to William Miller's, God sent someone to help him initiate his work, by extending an invitation to speak.

On Sunday Pastor J. B. Husted and several members of the Bromfield Street Second Methodist Episcopal Church, a White congregation, visited Foy and asked him to come to their house of worship and relate to them his visions. Apparently, eyewitness accounts of the supernatural phenomena that Foy had experienced had circulated in the community, to both Whites and Blacks, and people were interested in knowing about it. Sensing Foy's reticence, they went to his house to invite him in person.

Foy agreed and arranged to meet with them the following afternoon. He later recounted, "After they had left me, I regretted that such a step had been taken, and thought, had the world been mine, it would cheerfully be given to have the appointment recalled." His fears were still alive, but now he had committed himself. God must take care of the rest.

The auditorium of the Second Methodist Episcopal Church was said to comfortably seat about a thousand people. Foy reports: "The morning of the seventh, however, found my mind calm and peaceful; but as the hour for meeting drew nigh, temptations began sorely to afflict me. I feared lest my guide would not be with me and I should be unable to tell the people the things which had been shown me."[6]

When Monday morning dawned, Foy's mind was peaceful, but as the meeting time drew closer "temptations began sorely to afflict" him. he was afraid of being alone, afraid that he couldn't tell his story properly. Maybe he would be "unable to tell the people the things which had been shown [him]"; he was afraid of being intimidated, of being overwhelmed by the magnitude of the situation. The people, the setting, his color, the message, their reaction—all these factors exaggerated his fears.

But the people were aware of the struggle that Foy was experiencing, and were sympathetic: a band of church supporters went to his house and accompanied him to the meeting. Probably those were the longest 12 blocks that Foy had ever traveled. Arriving at the church, he faced a large congregation. People had crowded in to hear his account. With a bit of humor, Foy observed that "each individual seemed like a mountain."

Foy asked the pastor to open the meeting with prayer, hoping that they would have a prayer meeting instead. However, "while he was addressing the throne of grace," Foy relates, "It seemed as though I heard a voice speaking unto me and saying, 'I am with thee, and I promised to be with thee!'" At that moment Foy experienced true deliverance from his fears and insecurities. "My heart then began to burn within me, the fear of man suddenly fled," he says, "and unspeakable glory filled my soul." He described the receptiveness of the audience by saying, "I then related with great freedom the things shown me, while the congregation sat in perfect stillness."[7]

After this experience, Foy traveled for three months, delivering his message to full churches. Throughout this time, March to May 1842, he enjoyed "continual peace of mind." But then a fourth and final fear began to haunt him. Foy relates: "But after this I began to fear my family would come to want, and so went to work laboring with my hands, and thus continued for three months."[8]

Presumably, the trade skills he had learned earlier in life were put to use during this period, June to August. Of course, he was unable to travel during that time. However, God had other ways to provide for his needs. Foy states that while laboring, he "could find no rest day nor night, until again I consented to do my duty." So once again he started traveling, continuing to do so up to the time of the first printing of his book.

Foy, like other Advent preachers, sought invitations to speak. He experienced some persecution in his travels, but he quickly adds, "The promise of my guide has never failed." This was quite a testimony! Foy wanted all who read his pamphlet to know that he had kept his word when he said, "I will go," and that his guide had kept his promise, "I will be with thee." As a result, when writing his pamphlet in 1845, he could look back over the two-year period of traveling and sharing his messages and say of his guide, "his supporting presence has been with me."[9]

We can only approximate the time of Foy's third and fourth visions. The best reconstruction points to his receiving both visions during the summer of 1844. We do know that he received all of them before the Great Disappointment and that he traveled and shared them up to that time. We also know that we cannot agree with Loughborough's account that "he ceased public speaking" around 1845 and soon after "sickened and died."[10] We know that Foy lived until 1893, almost 50 more years, and that he continued to pastor, preach, and hold revivals up to the time of his death.

However, following the Great Disappointment, things were entirely different. The Millerite movement split up into small groups, and the teachings on the Second Coming didn't have the appeal they once had. Responding to the extreme confusion following the Great Disappointment, and in an effort to resolve the multitude of conflicting views, a number of Millerite leaders convened the Mutual Conference of Adventists at Albany, New York, in April 1845. Among other actions, the conference unanimously voted a report listing 10 "principles upon which we can unite."[11] One of these principles was a resolution expressing opposition to all claiming "special illumination." This, a legitimate reaction against fanaticism, effectively placed Foy and Ellen White outside the main remnant of the Millerite movement. It also impeded genuine manifestations of the Spirit.

Nevertheless, in line with his response to his guide, Foy continued to attempt to fulfill his commission in spite of all obstacles.

NOTES

[1] Foy, *Christian Experience,* p. 15.

[2] *Ibid.*

[3] *Ibid.*

[4] *Ibid.,* p. 24.

[5] *Ibid.,* p. 21.

[6] *Ibid.,* p. 22.

[7] *Ibid.*

[8] *Ibid.*

[9] *Ibid.,* p. 23.

[10] Loughborough, *The Great Second Advent Movement,* p. 147.

[11] Leroy Froom, *The Prophetic Faith of Our Fathers* (Washington, D.C.: Review and Herald Pub. Assn., 1954), Vol. IV, p. 834.goes on page 80

William Foy's tombstone located in the Birch Tree Cemetery in East Sullivan, Maine. On his tombstone is inscribed an appropriate epitaph: "I have fought a good fight . . ." (2 Timothy 4:7, 8).

CONCLUSION

"I have fought a good fight, I have finished my course, I have kept the faith: henceforth there is laid up for me a crown of righteousness, which the Lord, the righteous judge, shall give me at that day: and not to me only, but unto all them also that love his appearing."

2 Timothy 4:7, 8

Hazen Foss, the second to receive visions, refused to share what he had seen. He later referred to himself as "a lost man."

Hazen Foss: "He Refused to Obey"

The blistering effect of the Great Disappointment left the Advent movement in a daze. As F. D. Nichol eloquently put it: "For years the river of Millerism had flowed on in ever-increasing volume. It was no meandering stream, listlessly spreading over flat country for lack of sharply defined banks. There was a sense of urgency, of hastening toward a destination, that gave velocity and a sharply defined course to the river. Though there were eddies and swirls and crosscurrents and even marshy spots along the banks, these were mere incidentals. The main course and character of the stream were evident to all. Now the river of Millerism expected to be swallowed up in the ocean of eternity on October 22—Millerite charts marked out no land beyond that point." [1]

Advent believers were in a dilemma. Where were they to go? What were they to do now? The situation has been appropriately illustrated by the following: "A bicycle, even though the most unstable of conveyances, easily keeps its course as long as it is in motion. Indeed, the more rapid the motion, the easier it is to maintain the course. But let the forward motion cease, or only markedly decrease, and the rider finds himself more likely to suffer disaster, or at least to wander off the road, than to keep on the path he had set for himself.

And the likelihood of disaster is not decreased by the presence of more than one rider."[2]

Another illustration, appropriately applied to the Millerite movement following October 22, 1844, reads: "As long as it was truly a movement, it tended to hold all steadily to a course. But when the sudden halt came in October 1844, the inevitable happened. There was disaster for some, as they fell by the way, and a turning into bypaths for others. There were even collisions at times. The very fact that a new movement always draws in some who are inherently unstable and others whose chief quality is their ability to stand alone, or travel alone, only increased the spiritual traffic problem that confronted Millerism as 1845 opened."[3]

Yet in spite of the difficulty of this period, many still believed the Advent truths. Some who passed through this experience are recorded to have said, "We were perplexed and disappointed, yet did not renounce our faith. We felt that we had done our duty; we had lived up to our precious faith; we were disappointed, but not discouraged. We needed unbounded patience, for the scoffers were many."[4] And God empathized with His followers as they experienced this dark period.

The question may be asked, Where was God when all this took place? The answer is, God was where He has always been—with His followers. He was still in charge. No event catches Him off guard or finds Him unprepared. He allows events to unfold in a divinely preordained fashion. Yet to those who misunderstand His actions, He shows His compassionate concern in many reassuring ways.

In fact, shortly before the Great Disappointment God evidenced this concern in a signal manner. He made another attempt to prepare His followers by choosing yet another spokesman to sound forth the clarion call of providential guidance. Having used Foy as His sole prophetic spokesman for more than two and a half years, God selected another instrument to use. His choice in this second instance was a person entirely different from the first.

From a human standpoint, the second person selected to pick up the prophetic mantle differed from William Foy in many ways: he was a young White man; he was an Advent believer; he was socially acceptable; he was a good speaker; and he was well educated. He was well qualified, and his family also had strong connections with the Advent message. Of course, being White, he did not face the racial prejudice that Foy was regularly exposed to. His name was Hazen Foss, and he lived in Poland, Maine, about 30 miles from Portland.

Foss received his first vision in September or October of 1844. John Loughborough states that "a few weeks before the 'midnight cry' ended, the Lord came near and gave him a vision, in which he was shown the journey of the Advent people to the city of God, with their dangers."[5] Foss's vision corroborated that of William Foy, thus increasing the effectiveness of his message. In this same vision Foss was given a "view of the trials and persecution that would consequently follow if he was faithful in relating what had been shown him."[6] Here we have indication that his commission might have lasted for a prolonged period of time, like Ellen White's.

Like Foy, Foss was shown a vision of "three steps by which the people of God were to come fully upon the pathway to the Holy City."[7] Loughborough says that Foss, "being a firm believer in the Lord's coming 'in a few more days,' the part of the vision relating to the three steps onto the pathway was to him unexplainable; and being naturally of a proud spirit, he shrunk from the cross, and refused to relate it."[8]

Foss's defection is confirmed by Ellen White, as well as by Foss himself. Hazen Foss was indirectly related to Ellen White—his brother had married her sister Mary. In a letter to her sister dated December 22, 1890, Ellen said, "You know

Hazen Foss had visions once. He was firm in the faith that Christ would come in 1844. He interpreted the visions given him in harmony with his belief that time would close in 1844."[9] That he interpreted the vision in such a fashion was excusable. That he waited a few weeks before relating the vision—by which time the Great Disappointment had already passed—was also excusable. But Ellen White explains further, "After the time [the Great Disappointment] passed, he was told by the Lord to relate the visions to others. But he was too proud-spirited to do this. He had a severe conflict, and then decided he would not relate the visions."[10] In short, Foss refused his commission, and this was inexcusable.

Loughborough noted that the vision was "repeated the second time, and in addition he was told that if he still refused to relate what had been shown him, the burden would be taken from him and be given to one of the weakest of the Lord's children, one who would faithfully relate what God would reveal."[11] Nevertheless, he did refuse, and as Loughborough states, "a third vision was given, and he was told that he was released, and the burden was laid upon one of the weakest of the weak, who would do the Lord's bidding."[12]

Ellen White confirmed that when the people found out that Foss had received visions, they "assembled to hear him, but he refused." She elaborated: "I was told by one, in the presence of a room full, that they had urged Hazen Foss to tell them the things which the Lord had shown him. He had been greatly disappointed that the Lord did not come in 1844. He said that he had been deceived, and he refused to obey the promptings of the Spirit of God. After having plainly declared that he would not go from place to place and relate the visions God had given him, very strange feelings came to him, and a voice said, 'You have grieved away the Spirit of the Lord.'"[13]

When God released Foss from his commission, he was startled into action. He decided to make a belated attempt to relate what had been shown him, and made a public appointment for that purpose. We pick up Loughborough again: "The people crowded together to see and hear. He carefully related his experience, how he had refused to relate what the Lord had shown him, and what would result from his refusal. 'Now,' said he, 'I will relate the vision.' But alas! it was too late: he stood before the people as dumb as a statue, and finally said in the deepest agony, 'I cannot remember a word of the vision.' He wrung his hands in anguish, saying, 'God has fulfilled His word. He has taken the vision from me,' and in great distress of mind said, 'I am a lost man.'"[14]

Ellen White said of this meeting: "Those who gave a description . . . said it was the most terrible meeting they were ever in."[15]

Hazen Foss was later present at a meeting in which he heard a vision being related: "About three months from the time he failed to recall his vision, he heard from an adjoining room a vision related by another. The meeting was held in a dwelling-house where he was. He was urged to come into the meeting, but refused to do so. He said the vision was as near like that shown him as two persons could relate the same thing. And thus was known what he saw but could not remember when trying to relate it. On getting a view of the person afterward, he said, 'That is the instrument on whom the Lord has laid the burden.'"[16]

Who was this person that Foss saw? Who was the instrument on whom the Lord had laid the burden? It was a young lady named Ellen Harmon. She notes: "The next morning, I met Hazen Foss. Said he, 'Ellen, I want to speak with you. The Lord gave me a message to bear to His people, and I refused after being told the consequences. I was proud; I was unreconciled to the Disappointment. I murmured against God, and wished myself dead. Then I felt a strange feeling come over me. I shall be henceforth as one dead to spiritual things. I heard you talk last night. I believe the visions are taken from me, and given to you. Do not refuse to obey God, for it will be at the peril of your soul. I am a lost man. You are chosen of God; be faithful in doing your work, and the crown I might have had, you will receive.'"[17]

Following the rejection of his commission, despair seemed to be his lot. Foss lived some 50 years after this incident, but never again did he show any interest in spiritual things. Of his later experience, we read, "From that time he lost his hope in Christ, and went into a state of despair. He never attended an Adventist meeting again, and had no personal interest in religion. His demeanor in many respects, to say the least, has been that of one deprived of the gentle influence of the Spirit of the Master, of one 'left to his own ways, to be filled with his own doings.' In this condition of mind he died in 1893."[18]

We have now examined the experience of the second person to be given prophetic exposure. We can make some clear-cut conclusions from the experience of Hazen Foss as it compared with William Foy. First, God doesn't have to confine His activities and revelations to one person. He uses whomever He chooses, whenever He chooses, wherever He chooses, and however He chooses.

Second, God could have used Hazen Foss as effectively as He had used William Foy previously, and Ellen White subsequently, if Foss had been willing and cooperative.

Third, immediately before the Great Disappointment would have been an opportune time to establish a new spokesman for the Lord. Not only would he have offered prophetic guidance, but he also would have been in position to offer much-needed encouragement to God's people in the post-Disappointment period.

Fourth, though Foy was limited in his understanding and interpretation, his work with the Advent movement helped pave the way for the one who followed after him.

Many people today confuse Foy and Foss in person as well as in experience. But their work and their experiences were distinctly different, as may be seen by the following analysis:

1. Foy related the visions shown him; Foss didn't.

2. Foy anticipated redemption; Foss didn't.

3. Foy retained his Advent beliefs; Foss didn't.

4. Foy maintained his religious interest and church connections; Foss didn't.

5. Foy's experience was validated by others; Foss's wasn't.

NOTES

[1] Francis D. Nichol, *The Midnight Cry* (Washington, D.C.: Review and Herald Pub. Assn., 1944), p. 274.

[2] *Ibid.*, pp. 275, 276.

[3] *Ibid.*, p. 276.

[4] Loughborough, *The Great Second Advent Movement,* p. 187.

[5] *Ibid.*, p. 182.

[6] *Ibid.*

[7] *Ibid.*

[8] *Ibid.*

[9] Letter 37, 1890, in T. H. Jemison, *A Prophet Among You* (Mountain View, Calif.: Pacific Press Pub. Assn., 1955), p. 488.

[10] *Ibid.* Arthur Spalding remarks that "Foss was mindful of the strong sentiment against visions and dreams which had been built up in the Adventist ranks by the warnings and attitudes of the leaders. Without doubt the caution of Miller, Himes, Bliss, and others had secured the movement against extravagances. The fanaticism of John Starkweather in Boston and of C. R. Gorgas in Philadelphia, which were in part based upon pretended revelations, were examples of what might have been the fate of the Millerite movement had free rein been given to the most unstable elements. And Foss dreaded to put himself in the category of the dream prophets" *(Origin and History,* p. 57).

[11] Loughborough, p. 182.

[12] *Ibid.*

[13] Letter 37, 1890, in Jemison, pp. 488, 489.

[14] Loughborough, pp. 182, 183.

[15] Letter 37, 1890, in Jemison, p. 489.

[16] Loughborough, p. 183.

[17] Letter 37, 1890, in Jemison, p. 489.

[18] Loughborough, p. 183.

This photo of Ellen White (1904), taken at a special meeting at Oakwood College, Huntsville, Alabama, in which Blacks are also shown, is the only one of its kind.

The Baton Is Passed

In December 1844 Ellen Harmon (White) received her first vision, in Portland. From all indications, William Foy was also in the area. It is probable that he was aware of her experience and, in the light of his own, was especially interested. Foy was supportive of Ellen's receiving the prophetic gift. After hearing her relate her experience, he believed her to be the one whom God was using as His spokesperson for that time.

Shortly after Ellen had her first vision, Foy sought her out and expressed his desire to speak with her. Referring to this meeting, she said, "I had an interview with him."[1] We have no record of their conversation, but quite probably it dealt with her visions, what she had seen, and perhaps the accompanying physical phenomena. Most likely they discussed the relation of what they had seen to the Advent movement, the Disappointment, and the Second Coming.

Ellen had an appointment to speak on the evening following Foy's interview. Obviously he knew of the meeting, for although she didn't know that he was there, he was in attendance. Foy entered the meeting place, located a seat, and waited for her to speak. As she began, Foy became engrossed in what she was saying; he was caught up in the enthusiasm and pathos that accompanied her presentation. She talked of heavenly things—of guides, of lights, of imagery—things familiar to Foy. His heart responded with joy as he listened, lost to his surroundings. He began to relive the scenes of the better land. Never before had he heard anyone relate what he was hearing that night.

Caught up in the jubilance of the moment, he could hold back no longer. All of a sudden, right in the middle of Ellen's presentation, Foy let out a shout of joy, rose to his feet, and excitedly "jumped right up and down." As Ellen White remembered, "Oh, he praised the Lord, praised the Lord."[2]

He repeated again and again that her vision was just what he had seen. He knew there was no way to falsify such an experience—hers was legitimate.

The commotion drew the people's attention away from Ellen to Foy. He began sharing some of the things he had witnessed in vision that matched what she was relating. Ellen White noted, "They extolled him so I think it hurt him."[3] Whether she meant his pride was raised to the point it hurt his influence, is not spelled out. Perhaps the people's attention, their praise and compliments for what was an apparent confirmation of his visionary experience, completely embarrassed him. He had disrupted the meeting with his commotion; he had placed the speaker, who should have had the audience's attention, in an awkward position. He felt ill at ease and uncomfortable. With profuse apologies, he sought to calm things down and excused himself from the meeting. Ellen White concluded her account: "I do not know what became of him."[4]

It didn't take Foy long to grasp the situation. He had received visions and he had related what he had seen. Why then was another sharing things so similar to his messages? Was he still needed? Perhaps his commission was completed. Perhaps his work was done. He had been blessed to have visions. He had shared what had been shown him, though he did not understand all of it. Here was another who not only had

received visions—he could attest to that—but had the interpretation as well!

Foy's deep desire, as expressed in his pamphlet, was to
"comfort the saints." Now it was apparent that he would no
longer be the human conduit of that comfort. Yet he felt no
condemnation in the change. Considering his limitations, he
had done his best.

It was clear that in spite of the Disappointment, in spite of
the ridicule, scorn, and insults being levied against the Advent
believers, God had everything under control; He was still
leading those who trusted in His Word. Foy could breathe
easier.

With this conviction, Foy certainly didn't want to get in the
way, or hinder progress. He loved God and he loved God's
work, and he knew Ellen's experience to be genuine. The best
thing for himself, he felt, would be to move quietly off the scene
and continue his work in another part of the vineyard,
"waiting," as he had said, "for my coming Lord." The greatest
support he could give her, he believed, was to substantiate her
messages, as he had just done. He had his conversion experience and two of his visions published, for the "comfort of the
saints" and as a continuing testimony to his experience.
Though we now know where and how he spent his later years,
apparently the main body of Advent believers lost contact with
him. The baton had been passed!

NOTES

[1] Ellen White, "William Foy," Document File 231.
[2] *Ibid.*
[3] *Ibid.*
[4] *Ibid.*

Top: Frontal view of the Birch Tree Cemetery. The Foy marker is in the rear to the far right. Bottom: Tunk Pond not far from where the Foys lived is shown with Schoodic Mountain in the background.

A Comparison of Two Prophets

Let us now pause to examine William Foy's role and work as compared to that of Ellen White. It would be a mistake to confuse the roles of these two individuals. Just as John the Baptist's role was different from that of the apostle Paul, so William Foy's was different from Ellen White's. In the Bible there were different types of prophets, with different roles and functions. Compare the extended and varied ministry of Isaiah to the brief and limited role of Amos. But a prophet is one who serves as a mouthpiece, a spokesman, for God. David, a statesman/prophet, summed up the prophetic definition when he said, "The Spirit of the Lord spake by me, and his word was in my tongue" (2 Sam. 23:2).

Contrary to popular misconception, it seems clear that William Foy's role was not the same as that later filled by Ellen White. The two people stood at different foci of history, confronted with different circumstances and challenges. William Foy was a spokesman for God, largely to the Advent movement in the pre-Disappointment period. He was a herald and mouthpiece to the early Adventists, assuring them of God's personal interest, motivating them to greater revival and reformation, and bringing timely truths to view that would, if understood, spare His people the Great Disappointment or at least prepare them for it. Foy received a limited number of visions. He never suggested that his prophetic role was to extend past 1844, or that he was to receive more visions.

Here is where a misleading generalization is often made: that if Foy is accepted as a genuine prophet to the Advent movement (pre-Seventh-day Adventist), having received legitimate visions from God, he must also be a prophet to the Seventh-day Adventist movement as well. This belief, though understandable, is unsupported. Prophets, like people, have different functions. Peter was an early church leader, but he was not the missionary and theologian that Paul was. James was an apostle and early church administrator, but he didn't receive the revelations that John did. Martin Luther was a great reform leader, but he didn't fulfill the pastoral role that John Calvin did. William Miller preached God's message to the remnant—he was a burning and central light of the Advent movement—but he certainly didn't fill the foundational and organizational role that James White occupied in the early days of Seventh-day Adventism.

These were only men. Never perfect, they were sometimes painfully human; but each was sent to fulfill respective tasks for God. Our duty is to let them be what God intended them to be, and not try to fit them into other molds.

Is it not a masterstroke of divine wisdom for God to reach out to broaden the movement's sphere of influence and to reinforce its vitality by selecting many and varied leaders to carry the torch of truth? God never confines His work or secrets to a few. He uses selected leaders in signal ways, but His sovereign providence is neither limited nor parochial; it is worldwide. The use of more than one person in a latter-day prophetic role illustrates this divine prerogative.

What about the physical phenomena William Foy experienced during his visions? Although not every prophet experienced visions in exactly the same way. Daniel does describe something of his situation, in Daniel 10:8-19: loss of strength, falling to the ground, deep sleep, loss of breath. Similar phenomena were recorded of Ellen White on many occasions, by witnesses that included physicians.

The following excerpts describe Foy's experience:

1. Loss of strength. "I immediately fell to the ground, and knew nothing about this body."

2. No breath. "My breath left me." Dr. Cummings reported, "I examined him, but could not find any appearance of life, except around the heart."

3. Dumbness. "He dipped his hand into [water] and wet his forehead and his speech immediately came to him."

4. Strength returned. "The first appearance of life . . . was the raising of his right hand. . . . We wished him to tell us what things he had seen, and he answered, 'As soon as I receive my strength.'"

As there are similarities between Ellen White's experiences and those of William Foy, there are also many differences. Ellen White had a vast, multi-faceted work to perform, a work that included rebuke, warning, prediction, guidance, instruction, direction, protest, and strengthening. Her ministry lasted 70 years. Foy's prophetic ministry lasted approximately 2 years. William Foy served for a brief period *prior to* the Great Disappointment. Ellen White served for an extended period *after* the Great Disappointment.

It appears clear that both William Foy and Ellen White themselves understood the differences in their roles. Four aspects of their respective roles can be compared by considering how they viewed (1) the initiation, (2) the inclusiveness, (3) the purpose, and (4) the fulfillment of their work.

1. The initiation of their work.

William Foy: He consistently projected his work as specific and pointed, namely, to declare what he had seen and to warn others to flee from the wrath to come. He never gave any indication of viewing himself as a theologian, counselor, or founder of a new movement. Further, while he fulfilled a legitimate role as a prophet, like Ellen White, he never proclaimed himself a prophet. Both the title and closing words of his pamphlet convey the specific bounds of his work.

Ellen White: "I have had no claims to make, only that I am instructed that I am the Lord's messenger; that He called me in my youth to be His messenger, to receive His word, and to give a clear and decided message in the name of the Lord Jesus."[1] From the time of her earliest vision, Ellen White understood her work to be a lifelong calling.

2. The inclusiveness of their work.

William Foy: His guide told him, "Thou must reveal those things which thou has seen, and also warn thy fellow creatures to flee from the wrath to come. . . . I will go with thee, and support and help thee to declare these things unto the world."[2] That was his prophetic job description—to teach, preach, reveal, and warn. This was to cause a more thorough and lasting revival and reformation in the lives of the early Advent believers. In the course of fulfilling this task, he also performed other tasks, of course, but they weren't primary. Besides sparing many from experiencing the Great Disappointment, his reviving, reforming message would more thoroughly pave the way for the movement that was to follow.

Ellen White: "My Saviour declared me to be His messenger. 'Your work,' He instructed me, 'is to bear My word. Strange things will arise, and in your youth I set you apart to bear the message to the erring ones, to carry the word before unbelievers, and with pen and voice to reprove from the Word actions that are not right. Exhort from the Word.' . . . My work has covered so many lines that I cannot call myself other than a messenger, sent to bear a message from the Lord to His people, and to take up work in any line that He points out."[3]

William Foy functioned basically within a general sphere and time, while Ellen White's ministry covered the entire church life, over a broad period of time.

3. The purpose of their work.

William Foy: In particular he was to warn those who believed in the second advent of Christ (the "saints"). He appealed to sinners and backsliders as well.

Ellen White: "The Lord did not give to her long lines of prophecy, as He did to Daniel and to John the revelator; in these days just before the coming of the Lord new revelations of this kind would not be needed. He did not make her a judge and lawgiver as He did Moses, nor a ruler of state as He did Joseph and David. Rather, Mrs. White filled the position of a great teacher in Israel, as did Samuel; of a great reformer, as did Elijah; of a special messenger of God, as did John the Baptist." [4]

William Foy's focus was in the pre-Disappointment times with the early Advent movement. Ellen White's was in the post-Disappointment period with the Seventh-day Adventist movement.

4. The fulfillment of their work.

William Foy: His pamphlet ends on a positive and triumphant note: "My object in publishing these visions is to comfort the saints. They have been a great consolation to me in seasons of temptation and trial. Often, in the silent hours of the night, I have seemed to hear again the sweet song of the angels; and whenever my heart has felt sad and lonely, the things shown me by the angel have lifted me up above the trying scenes of earth. My desire is that the children of God may be blessed in the same manner. I am now waiting for my coming Lord. Although before the Lord was pleased to show me these heavenly things I was opposed to the doctrine of Jesus' near approach, I am now looking for that event. I expect soon to see the tall and mighty angel. 'Then shall I be satisfied when I awake in his likeness.' Ye saints of God, lift up your heads, for the glories of an earth made new will soon be yours." [5]

Foy closes his pamphlet with more Bible references and the

testimonials of some who witnessed him in vision. His final inclusion is a copy of his certificate of church membership, showing his involvement with a Christian church:

Copy of certificate of church
membership

This certifies that Bro. Wm. E. Foy is a regular member of the First Freewill Baptist Church in Augusta, in good standing. And as such, we commend him to the fellowship of the people of God, of every name, wherever he may chance to meet them.

Daniel Palmer
Church Clerk[6]

Foy's reputation and Christian witness in Maine during his later years are substantiated by ready testimonies of local inhabitants who had heard of him. Also, local histories record him as an "esteemed and beloved" preacher who held "meetings in the hall and also different schoolhouses."

Ellen White: Unquestionably, Ellen White also ended her work in a blaze of spiritual force. Her work was prolific, prodigious, and effective in every sense of the word. Between her first vision, concerning the struggles of the early Advent believers, in December 1844 and her last known divine manifestation, a prophetic dream concerning the welfare of the youth in the church on March 3, 1915, Ellen White had an estimated 2,000 visions and prophetic dreams. During seven decades of public work her literary output totaled more than 100,000 pages, or more than 25 million words. She wrote more books (60), published in more languages (more than 100), than any other woman in history; she is the fourth most translated writer in the world. Yet to the end she maintained her humility and dependence on God.

Ellen White remained active until she fell and fractured her hip while entering her study on Sabbath, February 13, 1915. A few weeks prior to her death she said, "I do not worry about the work I have done. I have done the best I could. I do not think that I shall be lingering long. I do not expect much suffering. I am thankful that we have the comforts of life in time of sickness. Do not worry. I go only a little before the others."[7]

Finally we read, "For several days prior to her death, she had been unconscious much of the time, and toward the end she seemed to have lost the faculty of speech and that of hearing. The last words she spoke to her son were 'I know in whom I have believed.'"[8]

William Foy's work was measured; Ellen White's was prolific. His prophetic ministry spanned a brief period; hers, almost three quarters of a century. Yet they both died feeling blessed to be used of God, content in having done their best, and looking forward to the resurrection.

NOTES

[1] Ellen White, in *Review and Herald,* July 26, 1906.

[2] Foy, *Christian Experience,* p. 20.

[3] White.

[4] E. G. White Estate, *The Spirit of Prophecy Treasure Chest* (Washington, D.C.: Review and Herald Pub. Assn., 1960), p. 10.

[5] Foy, p. 23.

[6] *Ibid.,* p. 24.

[7] Ellen White, *Life Sketches* (Mountain View, Calif.: Pacific Press Pub. Assn., 1915), p. 445.

[8] *Ibid.,* p.449

Top: An old cabin now stands on the spot where the Foy house was once located. Bottom: To the back of the old cabin is the well that the Foys dug when they first built on the spot.

Foy's Final Years

Foy's later years were quiet. Though he remained active in religious and pastoral work till the time of his death, his contributions were neither extraordinary nor theologically profound. In fact, following 1844, he spent his life in small rural communities, pastoring and doing personal missionary work.

There is little record of Foy's contact with the Advent believers following his final encounter with Ellen White. J. N. Loughborough actually thought that Foy had died, but he lived almost 50 years after the Disappointment.

Possibly Foy's absence from the public eye was because Advent preachers were not much in demand after the Disappointment. Many communities manifested a backlash against special illumination from God. Soon after the Great Disappointment, Foy and his family moved for a brief period from Portland, Maine, where he had met Ellen, to the Augusta area, where he reinvolved himself in the local church.

In Portland he had made acquaintance with the Pearson family, prominent Baptists. The sons, John and Charles, were the men who later published his pamphlet, *Christian Experience and Two Visions,* in 1845.

Foy's pamphlet fulfilled an important role. In it he shared his conversion experience and detailed two of the visions that he received. He documented his experiences in receiving visions and divine manifestations. What he did not do in the pamphlet is also important—he didn't publish the third vision that was like the one that Ellen White saw, nor did he get into theological or controversial issues. Still, in spite of popular feelings against visions and revelations, he made a strong case in behalf of the legitimacy of this gift of the Spirit.

Foy no doubt was acquainted with the emphasis of the Advent believers after the Disappointment. At the Low Hampton Conference of Adventists (December 28, 29, 1844) Joshua Himes urged three types of future missionary activities for the Advent believers to become involved in: "(1) comforting the saints who are still looking for the kingdom at hand; (2) arousing the professed Christian world once more to prepare for the Advent; (3) fully and freely proclaiming salvation to lost and perishing sinners."[1] Foy emphasized these in both his pamphlet and in personal activities. In print and in practice, he kept the embers of the Advent hope burning, presenting the teachings wherever he went.

Indications are that although he left Portland and moved to Augusta, he later went back to Portland to have his Christian experience printed by the Pearsons in the first half of 1845. His pamphlet was registered in the clerk's office of the district court of Maine. It was freely distributed to Advent believers and to anyone else who was interested.[2]

Sometime prior to 1850 his wife, Ann, and his father died, probably while he was living in the Augusta area. His daughter, Amelia, was still with him, and his mother, Betsy, came to live with him when her husband died. Foy must have deeply felt the loss of his wife, with whom he had shared his life and experiences for nearly 15 years.[3]

Sometime shortly before 1850 Foy received a call to pastor in New Bedford, Massachusetts, a port city located about 30 miles south of Boston. The census lists Foy as a Freewill Baptist pastor living in a Black neighborhood. The men of the community were predominantly sailors. At the time, New Bedford was the whaling capital of the world. Again Foy was assigned to a racially mixed congregation.[4]

During this period the Freewill Baptist Church was experiencing a shortage of pastors. Every available pastor was worked to the maximum, many having a number of churches in their district. During this time also the slavery issue rose more and more to the forefront. Freewill Baptists had taken a most courageous stand on behalf of the abolitionist movement, giving full support to the emancipation and betterment of Blacks. In 1849 the Freewill Baptists formed the Freewill Baptist Anti-Slavery Society; Silas Curtis, the pastor who baptized Foy, was the president (1849-1852).[5]

In 1851 Foy married Caroline Griffin, of Gardiner, Maine. A year later, while they were still living in New Bedford, a son was born to the new Foy family, whom they named Orrin. In 1855 Foy moved to pastor the Freewill Baptist church in Chelsea, Maine, a rural town a short distance from Augusta. Most of the congregations he pastored in Maine were either racially mixed or predominantly White. In 1856 a girl was born, who was given the name Lauraitta (Laura). Sadly, Caroline died in Chelsea, leaving William Foy with three young children. His mother was still living with them and she helped care for the children.[6]

In 1860 Foy moved to Burnham, Maine, about 100 miles north of Chelsea. There he boarded with a young farmer named Riley Whitten. Foy is again listed as a freewill Baptist clergyman, presumably serving a number of small congregations scattered throughout the area. It was a common practice for traveling preachers to board with local citizens, especially with Freewill Baptists. He is listed as owning a sizeable tract of land worth about $150, so he apparently had some means. Possibly he planned to settle there and was staying with the Whittens until he could clear land and build a house. But this did not happen, for three years later (1863) he moved farther east to an area sometimes referred to as South Maine.[7]

After some years in the active pastorate, during which time he filled a number of appointments, Foy moved to East Sullivan, Maine, in Hancock County, where he established permanent residence. This very rural settlement was referred to as Plantation No. 7 (early rural settlements not large enough to be townships were designated as plantations). There he bought property, built a house, and started a small farm. He also pastored a small congregation and conducted meetings in the local hall and schoolhouses.[8] "Elder Foy," as he was called, was greatly esteemed and loved in the area; verbal tradition has it that he was friendly and kind, yet of strong convictions. The local history declared Foy an excellent preacher and a skilled pastor. His personal care for his people revealed itself when Foy built a house for a neighboring family, and later helped build a church in the area.[9]

Tragedy struck again in 1863 when Laura, his 7-year-old daughter, who had recently begun to attend school, died. In 1870 his mother died at the age of 88. Amelia, his eldest daughter, had either married, moved away, or died before this time, as she was no longer listed in the census. So in 1870 Foy was living alone with his 18-year-old son, Orrin.[10]

Feeling a need for help and companionship, Foy returned to Portland sometime between 1870 and 1873, revived an old acquaintance, and returned to East Sullivan married to Parcentia Rose, a cook and housekeeper in the Portland area.[11] Upon his return, according to records of title deeds, Foy engaged in a number of land transactions. He bought land, and then sold it to his wife for a token amount. This was a common means of transferring land to a family member without having to go through probates and wills.

In 1880 William and Parcentia were still living in what

became Township No. 7. His name appears on a list of preachers in the area.

Elder William Foy died November 9, 1893, at 75 years of age. He was buried in Birch Tree Cemetery in East Sullivan, Maine. On his tombstone was inscribed as an appropriate epitaph the words of Paul found in 2 Timothy 4:7, 8:

> I have fought a good fight,
> I have finished my course,
> I have kept the faith:
> henceforth there is laid up
> for me a crown of righteousness.

William Foy was survived by his wife, Parcentia (d. December 24, 1908), and his son, Orrin (d. June 10, 1920). No descendants have been traced.

Thus we end the account of William Ellis Foy—prophet, preacher, pioneer. From the dusty annals of history emerges the account of one who deserves a place in both Advent and Seventh-day Adventist histories. The life lived, the words spoken, the records left, the work done, all leave us with the example of a life of worth. All Adventists may join in the hope that one day, when heaven's record is complete, they will meet William Foy in Paradise, the earth made new, which meant so much to him. "These all died in faith, not having received the promises, but having seen them afar off, and were persuaded of them, and embraced them, and confessed that they were strangers and pilgrims on the earth" (Heb. 11:13).

NOTES

[1] Damsteegt, *Foundations of the Seventh-day Adventist Message and Mission,* p. 113.

[2] Foy, *Christian Experience,* opening page and p. 24.

[3] 1860 U.S. Census, State of Maine, Cumberland County.

[4] 1850 U.S. Census, State of Massachusetts, Bristol County. This reasoning is also supported by an official genealogical search undertaken in connection with this writing project.

[5] See chapter 4.

[6] 1850, 1860 U.S. Census (Maine), *International Genealogical Index;* New Bradford Census Records (1850); Lydia Hinchman, *Early Settlers of Nantucket and Ancestors and Descendants.*

[7] 1860 U.S. Census (Maine).

[8] Johnson, *Sullivan and Sorrento Since 1760,* p.65

[9] *Ibid.,* p. 37.

[10] 1870 U.S. Census, State of Maine, Hancock County.

[11] *The Portland Directory and Reference Book* (1873), p. 223.

THE

CHRISTIAN EXPERIENCE

OF

WILLIAM E. FOY

TOGETHER WITH THE

TWO VISIONS

HE RECEIVED IN THE MONTHS OF JAN. AND FEB. 1842

PORTLAND:
PUBLISHED BY J. AND C. H. PEARSON.
1845.

REMARKS.

It is often remarked, when a work of this character, is before the public, "I am no believer in dreams and visions." Very well; such are welcome to their own discerning incredulity. The object in publishing these visions, is not to benefit such as reject indiscriminately every thing of this kind; no such expectations are cherished. But an earnest desire to comfort, and encourage the dear saints of God in their weary pilgrimage, by a glimpse of the blessedness, awaiting the finally faithful, has prompted us to this step. And no doubt is entertained but that it will prove to them, a rich, and invigorating repast.

That God does manifest himself, in visions to his children, the records of every age, do abundantly testify. And on this point, the Bible is clear and positive. The Patriarchs and Prophets were shown the great and mighty events, that were yet in the distant future, by the agency of visions. But it is often asked, if the method of revealing the events, and scenes of futurity, did not cease, when the dispensation of the spirit dawned. In reply, we would enquire, if this was the case, why then was the ushering in of the gospel age, so peculiarly marked by such manifestations? Revert to the scenes of Mount Tabor. The cloud of glory overshadowing the little band there assembled; how bright! how glorious! the appearence of the 'man of sorrows' as 'his face did shine as the sun,' and his raiment become 'white as the light'—how majestic! the appearence of Him who was carried to heaven in a fiery chariot, and Him whom God buried," and the voice of Jehovah speaking from the cloud, saying, "This is my beloved son—how overpowering! Well might the disciples "fall on their faces, being sore afraid!"

But why dwell upon a solitary case, when the bible reader has so many before him? Look at the case of a martyr Stephen, of a St. Paul, "caught up to the third heavens," of a John upon the isle of Patmos, and tell me if Jehovah has ceased to reveal himself in visions.

God, has in every age, thus dealt with the church; especially in seasons of tribulation. This was one way, in which the martyrs, were sustained, in their unparalleled sufferings. It was during their martyrdom, that Perpetia and Felicitas saw a ladder studded with swords, daggers, and instruments of torture, reaching from earth to heaven, at top of which stood Jesus Christ encourageing them

Nor are we wanting in instances of this kind in our day ; instances too, so clear and striking, as to be fully credited, by men of the greatest attainments, as well as the deepest piety. The extraordinary vision of Wm. Tennent, a Presbyterian Clergyman, in 1806 ; who, while he was conversing with his brother in Latin, fainted, and apparently died ; and was only saved from buriel, by the importunity of a friend; whenuse own language; "I heard and saw things all unutterable," is familiar to many.

Upon this subject the Bible is explicit; and those who truly have faith in the inspired word, are willing to let its testimony have full weight. Upon the day of Pentecost, when "the disciples were all filled with the Spirit, and, spake with other tongues," the multitude being amazed began to inquire; "What meaneth this?" And some said, "These men are filled with new wine." But Peter explains the matter; saying, "This is that &c." Now then, according to the prophecy of Joel as explained by St. Peter, the last days were to be peculiarly marked by these manifestations, so much so, as to become precursers of the great and notaable day of God.

The visions of our brother, are certainly very remarkable, and when related by him in public assemblies, have been blessed by God to the awakening of sinners, reclaiming of backsliders, and the building up of the saints in the most holy faith. They are published as nearly as possible in his own language. There is a most beautiful resemblance in the views here given, with the visions of Ezekiel, Daniel and John. As for instance; the description of the "tall and mighty angel," and "the sea of glass."

The view of the mighty angel having the trumpet of pure silver, and the announcement of the great and terrible voice, is exceedingly interesting and instructive.

That the despised and humble few, who are patiently waiting for the appearing of their glorious King, may be refreshed and comforted, in this hour of trial, while perusing these two visions, is the fervent prayer of the Publishers.

CHRISTIAN EXPERIENCE AND VISIONS

OF

WILLIAM E. FOY.

In the year 1835, under the preaching of Elder Silas Curtis, I was led to inquire, what I should do to be saved.

Christians, directed me to the Lamb of God, that taketh away the sins of the world. I then began to pray earnestly to God to pardon my sins ; but the more I prayed the more I beheld the sinfulness of my heart; and for many days I feared there was no mercy for me ; but was led to see, that it would have been justice in God, to have cut me off, and sent me where hope or mercy could not have reached me. I then became willing to give up all ; and in that moment Christ appeared the one altogether lovely, and the chiefest among ten thousands, and spake the life-giving word to my soul. I then rejoiced in the God of my salvation ; while all things around me appeared new, shining forth with the glory of God. Then could my heart unite in the song of the angels, "Glory to God in the highest, peace on earth, and good will towards men."   I then saw such a fulness in Christ, that I wanted to proclaim it to all the world.   O the glory of God that filled my soul! Three months rolled away in which I enjoyed sweet communion with my God.   I was then thrown into a trial by those who should have been nursing fathers in Israel, and thus remained many days, struggling in prayer; but the Lord knows how to deliver the godly out of temptation."   A father in Israel whom I visited at this time, gave me instruction that proved a blessing to my soul.   I then joined the Sabbath School, and was there instructed for the first time, to read the word of God, and soon became able to read my little bible.   Immediately the duty of baptism was impressed upon me; and after three months disobedience, I went before the church and related the dealings of God to my soul, and the day following was led down into the liquid stream by Bro. S. Curtis, and was buried with my Saviour in baptism.   Then did I experience the fulfillment of the promise; "They that wait upon the Lord shall renew their strength; they shall mount up as on wings of eagles, run and not be weary, walk and not faint;" and while coming up out of the water, it appeared to me the opening heavens around me shone; and I cried with a loud voice, saying: " Glory to God, and the

Lamb that sitteth upon the throne!"

On the 18th of January, 1842, I met with the people of God in Southark St., Boston, where the christians were engaged in solemn prayer, and my soul was made happy in the love of God. I was immediately seized as in the agonies of death, and my breath left me; and it appeared to me that I was a spirit separate from this body. I then beheld one arrayed in white raiment, whose countenance shone beyond the brightness of the stars, and a crown was upon his head which shone above the brightness of the sun.

This shining one, took me by my right hand, and led me upon the bank of a river; in the midst, was a mount of pure water. Upon the bank, I beheld a multitude, both great and small; they were the living inhabitance of the earth. Soon all moved towards the west, walking on the water, until we reached the mount. This became the separating line between the righteous and the wicked. The righteous crossed it, passed through three changes; 1st, their bodies were made glorious. 2d, they received pure and shining garments. 3d, bright crowns were given them.

But when the wicked reached the spot where the righteous were changed, they cried for mercy, and sank beneath the mount. The saints then passed on to a boundless plain, having the appearence like pure silver. Our guide then spake and said, *This is the plain of Paradise.'*

This heavenly host.was then divided into flocks, some, exceeding large in number, others, but small. In the middle of each was an angel. These angel's garments, were pure and white and unto each of them,was given a crown,shining with great brightness. Their countenances were most lovely to behold; their wings like unto flaming fire, beneath which were the saints, both small and great. The guide, then said, "*These angels are they that have preached the gospel on the earth.*" I then beheld as it were a great gate before me. The gate was so tall, the height thereof I was unable to see. Before the gate stood a tall and mighty angel clothed in raiment pure and white; his eyes were like flaming fire, and he wore a crown upon his head, which lighted up this boundless plain. The angel raised his right hand, and laid hold upon the gate, and opened it; and as it rolled upon its glittering hinges, he cried with a loud voice, to the heavenly host, *You r all welcome!*" Then, the guardian angels, in the midst of the saints, struck a song of triumph, and the saints, both small and great sang with loud voices, and passed within the gate; and the guardian angels arose upon their glittering wings, and vanished from my sight. The inside of the gate, appeared like glittering diamonds. Beneath our feet, was as the appearance of pure glass. I then beheld, countless millions of shining ones, coming with cards in their hands. These shining ones become our guides. The cards they bore, shone above the brightness of the sun; and they placed them in our hands; but the names of them, I could not read. These guides took us by the right hand, and led us to a boundless place. Then I lifted mine eyes, and looked above, no clouds, or skies appeared; but there, countless millions of bright angels, whose wings were like unto pure gold; and they sung with loud voices, while their wings cried *"Holy! Holy!"* I then beheld an innumerable multitude, arrayed in white raiment, with cards upon their breasts; and unto each was given a crown of brightness. The guide spake, saying, *"These are they which have passed through death."*

There was arrayed before me in the spirit, an innumerable multitude, which had not passed through death; their crowns were like the brightness of the stars; and in their right hands the held cards. I then saw an individual, which had passed through death. Her brightness was beyond the expression of mortals, and at her right side stood a guardian angel; the angel's raiment was like pure gold, and his wings like flaming fire, and as she passed me, she cried with a lovely voice, *"I am going to the gate to meet my friends"* An angel then appeared flying through the midst of this boundless place, and came to the spirit of one of those which had not passed through death, and cried with a loud voice, saying, " *This is my Mother.*" He then became her guide. I then beheld in the midst of this boundless place a high mountain like unto pure silver. It appeared perfectly round, and although I was unable to see through it, yet my vision extended around it. Around this mountain was a space in which stood no being. But after this vacant circle, stood as it appeared to be, a choir of angels, and as far as my sight could extend, throughout this boundless place, stood the countless millions of the righteous. And O! the singing no mortal can describe! It appeared to me, the angels next to the circle around about the mountain, with loud voices struck a lovely song, and then ceased. The saints next to them caught the strain, and with voices yet more loud, repeated it; and thus it echoed, and re-echoed, until it had been sung by all the saints, and then it ceased: and then again the angels sang.

At the right side of the mountain, appeared a mighty angel, with raiment like unto burnished gold, his legs were like pillars of flaming fire, his countenance was like the lightning, and his crown gave light to this boundless place, and those that had not passed through death, could not look upon his countenance. I then beheld upon the side of this mount, letters like pure gold, which said, *"THE FATHER, AND*

THE SON." Directly under these letters stood the mighty angel, whose crown lighted up the place, and all the heavenly host worshiped at his feet, round about the mountain. This mighty angel then raised his right hand, which appeared like a flaming sword, and all the multitude of those that had not passed through death, were caught up to the top of the mountain ; and there was a large book opened, and their names came up out of the book in the form of cards, which were stamped upon their fore-heads.

We then stood again upon this pure sea of glass, before the mountain ; and our bodies had become like transparent glass ; but the being that was within the mountain, I was unable to behold. While I was gazing upon the glories before me, a great voice spake in the mountain, and the place was mightily shaken, and the countless multitudes of saints and angels, bowed at the feet of the mighty angel, and worshiped him crying with a loud voice' *"Hallelujah"*! and then every voice was hushed, and the heavenly host remained bowed before the angel in solemn silence ; and nought was heard save the trembling of the place caused by the voice of him who spake in the mount.

I then beheld this lower world, wrapt as it were in rolling mountains of flame. and in this fire,I saw a countless multitude crying for *mercy*. They appeared to be the aged and those who had come to the years of understanding. Their cries came up before the mountain, while all the heavenly host were bowed in solemn stillness. The voice from the mountain, spake again, and all the saints and angels arose, and with loud voices cried *"AMEN."*

I then began to converse with my guide, and inquired, *why there was no mercy for those, whom I had seen in distress.* He answered, *"The gospel has been preached unto them, and the servants have warned them, but they would not believe; and when the great day of God's wrath comes, there will be no mercy for them.*

I then beheld in the middle of this boundless place a tree, the body of which, was like unto transparent glass, and the limbs were like transparent gold, extending all over this boundless place. On every branch of the tree, were small angels standing. There was an innumerable multitude of them, and they sung with loud voices, and such singing has not been heard this side of heaven This tree was also clothed in light proceeding from the mighty angel. Beneath this tree standing on the sea of glass, were the countless millions of the righteous, arrayed in white raiment, with crowns on their heads, and cards upon their breasts; and in the multitude I saw some that I knew while they were living upon the earth, and they we all singing with loud voices and ifting up their glittering hands plucking fruit from the tree; the fruit appeared like clusters of grapes in pictures of pure gold. With a lovely voice, the guide then spoke to me and said *"Those that eat of the fruit of this tree, return to earth no more."* I raised my hand to partake of the heavenly fruit, that I might no more return to earth; but alas! I immediately found myself again, in this lonely vale of tears.

The duty to declare the things which had thus been shown me, to my fellow creatures, and warn them to flee from the wrath to come, rested with great weight upon my mind; but I was disobedient, settling upon this point for an excuse, that my guide did not command me so to do; and I thereby, brought darkness, and death, upon my soul. But I could find no peace or comfort. I began to doubt whether indeed my soul had ever been converted, and although i often met with the people of God, I obtained no relief, but felt distressed and lonely. I could get no access in prayer. At last in order to escape the cross of going and personally declaring it to the world, I decided to have it printed. Yet, in this I could find no relief. Besides after having an account of it printed, it was a very imperfect sketch; and indeed I was unable to relate it for that purpose. But the Lord in his mercy spared me to behold the evnmg of the 4th of Feb. 1842, when I met with the people of God in May St. A large congregation was gathered together, and

christians were engaged in exortation and prayer.   But I enjoyed none of the sensible presence
of God.

In the last part of the evening, the house being much crowded, I gave my seat to a friend
who had been standing through the evening.
While I was thus standing, I began to reflect
on my disobedience; and while thus engaged,
suddenly I heard a voice, as it were, in the
spirit, speaking unto me.   I immediately fell
to the floor, and knew nothing about this body,
until twelve hours and a half. had passed away,
as I was afterwards informed.

It appeared to me that I was a spirit separate
from this body, standing upon the earth alone.
No other being appeared to be with me.   The
earth had the appearance of a place perfectly
level. The sun shone forth in its splendour, as
it naturally does at noon day.   I then beheld a
cloud gently rising out of the west, which came
up and covered the sun, so that it was darkened,
and the whole heavens become like sackcloth;
then something beyond the expression of mortal
man, barst forth from the heavens, from the
south even unto the north.   It was like a flaming bar of fire; and immediately after, something appeared, which it is impossible for me
to describe.   I then beheld innumerable multitudes coming from the four quarters of the
earth and were assembled before this bar, and
there stood in solemn silence, while paleness

gathered on all countenances. Immediately they were caught up to this bar, and the bodies of the saints were changed, becoming like transparent gold; and they were clothed in light and shining garments, and crowns of brightness were placed upon their heads, and shining cards upon their breasts; and singing sweetly, they passed through the bar of fire. But the wicked were unable to pass. The world beneath appeared to be wrapt in darkness and fire; into this, the wicked sunk from my sight, crying for mercy. I beheld mothers with their infants in their arms come to the flaming bar; the bodies of the infants become like transparent gold, and on wings of flaming fire, they passed the bar, singing with lovely voices, and the unholy mothers, crying for mercy, would sink below.

I then beheld an innumerable multitude coming up from the waters, and an innumerable multitude, coming up out of the earth, arrayed in white raiment, with cards upon their breasts, and singing with loud voices, they passed this bar, and received crowns of glory upon their heads.

I then beheld, a multitude coming up out of the earth, and some of them I knew whose names were enroled in the church books on earth, some of whom I had seen communing with the saints of different orders, and some which had professed to be preachers of the gospel. Although they had high professions, yet they were not found worthy, but cried for mercy, and sunk with those who had blasphemed. As we passed the bar, we entered upon a boundless place which was lighted up with great brightness. Near the place through which we passed. I beheld a mighty angel clothed in pure white raiment, having a crown of brightness on his head. He appeard to be gazing through the bar, and his eyes like lamps of fire were fixed with steadfastness upon the earth. He stood with his right foot placed before him, as though walking; and his object appeared to be, to reach the earth. But three steps remained for him to take. Against his breast, and across his left hand, was as it were, a trumpet of pure silver; and a great and terrible voice came from the midst of the boundless place, saying, *"The sixth angel hath not yet done sounding"* Behind the angel, I beheld countless millions of bright chariots, they had the appearance of pure gold, and were perfectly square. Each chariot had four wings like flaming fire. And while I was beholding, one of the chariots arose upon its wings of fire, and an angel followed after the chariot; and the wings of the chariot, and the wings of the angel, cried as with one loud voice, saying, *"Holy! Holy!"* I watched the chariot, listening to the lovely sound of the wings. It passed towards the earth; and there appeared a spirit, arrayed in white raiment as it were, standing upon a mountain, and there was given him a crown of brightness ; and he stepped into the chariot with the angel, and in a moment he was in this boundless place. Although he shone with great brightness yet this individual I knew, it was the one refered to by the witness * who said, "I see the chariot coming!" He departed this life, in just two weeks after I saw him in vision.

I then saw in the midst of the place, an innumerable multitude, arrayed in white raiment, standing in a perfect square, having, crowns of unfading glory upon their heads. They were of the size of children ten years of age; and they sung a song, which the saints and angels could not sing. In the midst of this boundless place, there was a river of pure water, and on either side of the river, countless millions of angels stood, with crowns of brightness upon their heads ; they had in their hands cups like pure gold, and were bowing down and partaking of the water of the river, singing with loud and lovely voices, and worshiping him, whose crown gave light, to this boundless place.

Then came one unto me clothed in white, whom I call my guide ;— he led me to a place

---

* Mary Black, the wife of the deceased Eld. George Black (the individual seen in the vision) testifies, "These are his dying words, 'I see the chariots coming to waft my spirit home.' He then left the world with a shout."

like unto a narrow door. The first which I beheld, was a mighty angel, upon the right hand, having a large book open before him, also at the left, another with a book open before him . my guide, then spake to me, saying, *They that repent of their sins on the earth, are blotted out of the book on the left, and recorded on the right .*" I then beheld angels ascending and descending too and from the earth ; they bore tidings to the recording angels .

My guide, now, informed me what I must do; saying, "*Thy spirit must return to yonder world, and thou must reveal those things which thou hast seen, and also warn thy fellow creatures, to flee from the wrath to come .*" I then answered him saying, "*How can I return to yonder world ?* "He answered me ; *I will go with thee, and support and help thee, to declare these things unto the world .*" Then, I answered the angel,— *I will go .*

I then beheld this lower world. It seemed as though the vail which had separated it, from the boundless place in which I stood, was removed, and they had both become as one ; and the saints and angels were continuilly passing from, and to, the earth . The earth appeared like a calm sea of transparent gold ; above no cloud or sky appeared, but the air was perfectly pure, and of a silvery brightness. I then heard all the saints, and angels, in heaven, and on the earth, singing with loud voices. My guide then spread his wings, and brought my spirit gently to the earth, then soared away; and immediately I found myself in the body.

Notwithstanding the command of my guide, and my solemn promise to declare these things to the world; I was at first exceedingly unwilling so to do, and it was three days, before I revealed them in a public manner.

The message was so different–and the manner in which the command was given, so different from any I had ever heard of, and knowing the prejudice among the people against those of my color, it became very crossing.

These questions were continually arising. Why should these things be given to me, to to bear to the world, and not to the learned, or to one of a different condition from myself? But no peace could I obtain in disobedience. "Woo is me if I declare not these things," rested heavily upon my soul.

On the 6th of Feb, the Pastor of the Broomfield St. Church, called upon me, and requested me to relate my visions in his house of worship. Several members of that church were present, and were anxious for me to comply. I consented; and the appointment was made for the next afternoon. After they had left me I regretted that such a step had been taken, and thought had the world been mine it would cheerfully be given, to have the appointment recalled.

The morning of the 7th, however, found my mind calm and peaceful; but as the hour for meeting drew nigh, temptations began sorely to afflict me. I feared lest my guide would not be with me, and I should be unable to tell the people, the things which had been shown me. A band of brethren, sympathising with me accompanied me to the meeting. Upon entering the house, I found a large congregation assembled, and each individual, seemed like a mountain. So much of the fear of man, rested upon me, that I asked the Pastor, to open the meeting with prayer; telling him, I thought they would be obliged to have a prayer meeting. But while he was addressing the throne of grace it seemed as though I heard a voice, speaking unto me, and saying, *"I am with thee ; and I promised to be with thee!"*my heart then began to burn within me, the fear of man suddenly fled, and unspeakable glory filled my soul. I then related with great freedom, the things shown me, while the congregation sat in perfect stillness. From this time I traveled three months delivering my message to crowded houses, enjoying continual peace of mind. But after this I began to fear my family would come to want, and so went to work laboring with my hands, and thus continued for three months. But I could find no rest day nor night, until again I consented to do my duty. Since then. I have traveled from place to place, and suffered some persecution, but the promise of my guide has never failed. His supporting presence has been with me.

My object in publishing these visions, is to comfort the saints. They have been a great consolation to me, in seasonsof temptation and trial.

Often, in the silent hours of the night, I have seemed to hear again, the sweet song of the angels ; and whenever my heart has felt sad and lonely, the things shown me by the angel, have lifted me up above the trying scenes of earth.

My desire is, that the children of God, may be blessed in the same manner. I am now waiting for my coming Lord. Although before the l ord was pleased to show me these heavenly things, I was opposed to the doctrine of Jesus' near approach, I am now looking for that event. I expect soon to see the tall and mighty angel. "Then shall I be satisfied, when I awake in his likeness."

Ye saints of God, lift up your heads, for the glories of an earth made new,will soon be yours.

"Eye hath not seen, nor ear heard, neither have entered into the heart of man, the things which God hath prepared for them that love him." "But God hath revealed them unto us by his spirit; for the spirit searcheth all things, yea, the deep things of God."

TESTIMONIALS.

We, the undersigned, inhabitance of Boston, were witnesses of the apparently inanimate condition into which our brother, Wm. Ellis Foy, was thrown from some unknown cause, on the 18th of January 1842, when he laid two hours and a half; and again Febuary 4th, when he laid twelve hours and a half, during which, each time, he testifies that he experienced extraordinary visions of another world.

Charles Tash.	Francis Sanders.
George Williams.	John Thomas.
David Williams.	Andrew Lewis.
Edward Williams.	George Harris.

Dr. Henry Cummings, testifies: "I was present with our brother at the time of his visions. I examined him, but could not find any appearance of life, except around the heart."

Ann Foy testifies: "The first appearence of life I saw in him, was the raising of his right hand. He then arose upon his knees, and made signs for water, which was given him. He dipped his hand into it, and wet his forehead, and his speech immediately came to him. We then wished him to tell us, what things he had seen, and he answered, as soon as I receive strength, I will reveal unto you, that which the Lord has revealed unto me."

Copy of certificate of church membership.

This certifies that Bro. Wm. E. Foy, is a regular member, of the first Freewill Baptist Church, in Augusta, in good standing. And as such, we commend him to the fellowship of the people of God, of every name, whereever he may chance to meet them.

DANIEL PALMER,
Church Clerk.

Egypt's Land
By William E. Foy

When I was down in Egypt's land,
I heard my Savior was at hand,
And the midnight cry was sounding,
And I wanted to be free,
So I left my formal brethren
To sound the Jubilee.

They said that I had better stay,
And go with them in their own way,
But they scoffed at my Lord's power,
With them I could not agree,
So I left their painted synagogues
To sound the Jubilee.

They call us now a noisy crew,
And say, they hope we'll soon get through,
Be we now are growing stronger,
Both in love and unity,
Since we left old mystic Babylon
To sound the Jubilee.

When Satan comes to tempt your minds,
Then meet him with these blessed lines,
Saying, get behind me, Satan,
I have naught to do with thee,
I have got my soul converted,
And I'll sound the Jubilee.

The battle is not to the strong—
The weak shall sing the conqueror's song,
I've been through the fiery furnace,
And no harm was done to me,
I came out with stronger evidence
To sound the Jubilee.

Hallelujah, Hallelujah, Hallelujah,
I am free—from all sectarian prejudice,
To sound the Jubilee!

Ellen G. White
on William Ellis Foy

Ellen G. White: We used to have some very powerful meetings. But it is not all out there, and I don't know as there is any need of putting it out.

Elder Stockman was preaching, and he was dying with the consumption. He talked as though inspired by the Holy Spirit, feeble as he was. I always sat on the front seat next to the stand, and as I heard a noise like a groan I saw that Elder Brown was as white as human flesh could be, and he was falling out of his chair. I suppose my interested look to him called the attention of Stockman, and he looked around, and he [Brown] was ready to fall on the floor. He [Stockman] turned around, and said, "Excuse me," and took him in his arms, and laid him down on the lounge. He was one that did not believe in these things, and he had a taste of it right there. The power of the truth came upon him so. . . .

Then another time, there was Foy that had had visions. He had had four visions. He was in a large congregation, very large. He fell right to the floor. I do not know what they were doing in there, whether they were listening to preaching or not. But at any rate he fell to the floor. I do not know how long he was [down]—about three quarters of an hour, I think—and he had all these [visions] before I had them. They were written out and published, and it is queer that I cannot find them in any of my books. But we have moved so many times. He had four.

Dores Robinson: Did you ever have an interview with him?

Ellen G. White: I had an interview with him. He wanted to see me, and I talked with him a little. They had appointed for me to speak that night, and I did not know that he was there. I did not know at first that he was there. While I was talking I heard a shout, and he is a great, tall man, and the roof was rather low, and he jumped right up and down, and oh, he praised the Lord, praised the Lord. It was just what he had seen, just what he had seen. But they extolled him so I think it hurt him, and I do not know what became of him.

His wife was so anxious. She sat looking at him, so that it disturbed him. "Now," said he, "you must not get where you can look at me when I am speaking." He had on an Episcopalian robe. His wife sat by the side of me. She kept moving about and putting her head behind me. What does she keep moving about so for? We found out when he came to his wife. "I did as you told me to," said she. "I hid myself. I did as you told me to." (So that he should not see her face.) She would be so anxious, repeating the words right after him with her lips. After the meeting was ended, and he came to look her up, she said to him, "I hid myself. You didn't see me." He was a very tall man, slightly colored. But it was remarkable [the] testimonies that he bore.

I always sat right close by the stand. I know what I sat there for now. It hurt me to breathe, and with the breaths all around me I knew I could breathe easier right by the stand, so I always took my station.

Dores Robinson: Then you attended the lectures that Mr. Foy gave?

Ellen G. White: He came to give it right to the hall, in the great hall where we attended, Beethoven Hall. That was quite a little time after the visions. It was in Portland, Maine. We went over to Cape Elizabeth to hear him lecture. Father always took me with him when we went, and he would be going in a sleigh, and he would invite me to get in, and I would ride with them. That was before I got any way acquainted with him.

Dores Robinson: Where did you see him first?

Ellen G. White: It was there, at Beethoven Hall. They lived near the bridge where we went over to Cape Elizabeth, the family did.

White, Ellen G. "Interview With Mrs. E. G. White Regarding Early Experiences."
Manuscript 131, 1906, pp. 1, 4, 6. In Ellen G. White. *Manuscript Releases.*
Silver Spring, Md.: Ellen G. White Estate, 1993, vol. 17, pp. 95-97.

Occasion

Before Ellen White's death a series of interviews concerning her life were undertaken to be used as material for a book, most likely *Life Sketches of Ellen G. White,* published in 1915. In this lengthy interview on August 13, 1906, in White's home called Elmshaven in California's Napa Valley, White and Robinson cover supernatural phenomena during the Millerite years. Much of the material was not included in *Life Sketches* and largely remains unpublished to this day.

Participants

Interviewer: Dores Eugene Robinson (1879-1957) first worked as a secretary for Ellen White in the late 1890s when both lived in Australia, and continued in her employ in the United States on and off until her death in 1915.

Interviewee: Ellen Gould Harmon White (1827-1915) was a co-founder and prophet of the Seventh-day Adventist Church.

Places

Beethoven Hall

"He came to give it right to the hall, in the great hall where we attended, Beethoven Hall."

"Musical culture in Portland [Maine] began with Edward Howe in 1805. He became the founder of the Beethoven Musical Society. In 1824 the society established its own music hall. For a time it had a 'small, but remarkably sweet toned organ of its own.' When the society disbanded in 1826, the organ was purchased by Howe and relocated to his home. In 1829 a new organization formed—the Handel and Haydn Society. Meetings were held in Beethoven Hall, which seated about 200 people.

"Adventists held meetings in Beethoven Hall following William Miller's 1840 meetings in the Casco Street Christian Church. This continued at least into 1845. Beethoven Hall was located on the third floor of a building on the east side of Congress Street near the head of Center Street near where Middle Street branches from Congress.

"Ellen White wrote of the meetings:

"'Notwithstanding the opposition of ministers and churches, Beethoven Hall, in the city of Portland, was nightly crowded; especially was there a large congregation on Sundays. All classes flocked to these meetings. Rich and poor, high and low, ministers and laymen, were all, from various causes, anxious to hear for themselves the doctrine of the second advent. Many came who, finding no room to stand, went away disappointed.

"'The order of the meetings was simple. A short and pointed discourse was usually given, then liberty was granted for general exhortation. There was, as a rule, the most perfect stillness possible for so large a crowd. The Lord held the spirit of opposition in check while His servants explained the reasons of their faith. Sometimes the instrument was feeble, but the Spirit of God gave weight and power to His truth. The presence of the holy angels was felt in the assembly, and numbers were daily added to the little band of believers' (*Life Sketches* [1915], p. 54).

"Matthew F. Whittier, 'the younger brother of the Quaker poet John Greenleaf Whittier and a resident of Portland, visited a Millerite meeting in Beethoven Hall during September 1844.' He was not a 'believer' and so is somewhat cynical in his choice of words. Nevertheless, he provides some interesting insights on the meetings and the Hall.

"'With considerable difficulty, on account of the crowd, we ascended the two flights of dark and dirty stairs, and . . . elbowed our way into the hall. A motley crowd of all sizes, shapes, conditions and collors [*sic*] filled the hall and its galleries. . . . Clustered around a rude rostrum were the elect; most of them were in a kneeling posture. . . .

"'Around the hall hung pictures of strange uncouth animals, supposed to be the representation of those seen by Daniel and by St. John at Patmos' (F. Whittier, in Portland *Transcript*, Nov. 1, 1945 [*sic*], p. 228)" (Merlin D. Burt, *Adventist Pioneer Places: New York & New England* [Hagerstown, Md.: Review and Herald Pub. Assn., 2011], pp. 40, 41).

Cape Elizabeth

"We went over to Cape Elizabeth to hear him lecture."

Cape Elizabeth is a town in southern Maine incorporated on November 1, 1765, abutting South Portland on the Atlantic Ocean. The town's most famous attraction is the Portland Head Lighthouse, completed in 1791 by order of George Washington, making it the oldest lighthouse on Casco Bay. The Foys resided next to Portland Harbor either on the Cape Elizabeth or South Portland side.

Portland

"It was in Portland, Maine."

Portland was Maine's first capital city, situated on the state's southwestern coast. Because of its strategic location, Portland became a vital international commercial seaport and land transportation depot, giving the city a cosmopolitan status. Ellen White was born near Portland in 1827, and the Harmons moved to the larger city shortly after her birth, where she spent the remainder of her adolescence. William Foy and his family moved to Portland sometime around 1842. Portland's 1840 population was just above 15,000.

Definitions

"But they extolled him [William Foy] so I think it hurt him, and I do not know what became of him."

Extolled: "Exalted in commendation; praised; magnified" (*Webster's International Dictionary of the English Language* [1900]).

John N. Loughborough
on William Ellis Foy

Loughborough, J. N. *Rise and Progress of the Seventh-day Adventists*. Battle Creek, Mich.: General Conference of Seventh-day Adventists, 1892, pp. 70, 71.

While this work of expulsion was going on in the churches, and the loud cry of the message was swelling its notes all over the world, the Lord came near to the comfort of His people by a special manifestation of the gift of His Spirit. There was an educated mulatto in the State of Massachusetts, by the name of Foye, who was an eloquent speaker. He was a Baptist, but was preparing to take holy orders as an Episcopal minister. The Lord graciously gave him three visions, which bore clear evidence of being the genuine manifestations of the Spirit of God. He was invited from place to place to speak in the pulpits, not by the Episcopalians only, but by other denominations. When he spoke, he always wore the clergyman's robe, such as the ministers of that church wear in their services. His visions related to the near advent of Christ, the travels of the people of God to the heavenly city, the new earth, and the glories of the redeemed state. Having a good command of language, with fine descriptive powers, he created a sensation wherever he went. There was one thing, however, in the vision of the pathway of God's people that he did not understand; and that was three steps leading up onto this pathway, such steps of glorious light that he called them "steps of fire." On each of these steps was a great multitude of people; but suddenly many of them disappeared, while those who remained passed onto the second step, where a multitude gathered also; and some of these disappeared, and so on with each advancing step. Those who disappeared seemed to sink down into the step, and were seen no more. He saw the people of God, those who remained, pressing on with joy over the heavenly pathway. This was the part of the vision that troubled him.

After Mr. Foye had traveled awhile in various parts of New England, he had his visions printed in a pamphlet, entitled "Foye's Visions." He finally became exalted over the revelation, and thus lost his simplicity, hence the manifestation of this gift to him ceased, and soon after he sickened and died.

Loughborough, J. N. "The Study of the Testimonies—No. 4." *General Conference Daily Bulletin*, Jan. 31, Feb. 1, 1893, p. 59.

God began to manifest this gift [the spirit of prophecy] in the first message, before the time passed [October 22, 1844], as early as 1842. William Foye, of Boston, was given three visions, showing the pathway of the Advent people; and he went from place to place relating them. He saw the people being brought on to three different platforms, one following another. Some dropped through the first and went out of sight, and the others went on to the second one. Some dropped through this and disappeared, and the remainder went to the third. Still others disappeared through this, and then the remainder went on to the city of God. In another vision he saw a mighty angel come down from heaven, and a voice cried and said, "This angel has yet three steps to take." He [Foy] didn't understand anything about it; but is there any one here to-day who doesn't know what that meant? He lived to hear Sister Harmon relate her first vision, and to testify that the two were identical.

Loughborough, J. N. "The Prophetic Gift." *Review and Herald*, July 18, 1899, p. 2.

About 1833, but more especially since 1840, a message has been sounding through the earth proclaiming the coming of Christ near at hand, "even at the door." In connection with this proclamation the Lord has been pleased to manifest the power of His Spirit in various ways, and in a marked manner. In many instances, not only in America, but in other lands, the Lord has been gracious to His people who have been engaged in heralding the glad tidings of our returning Lord, by speaking to them through the gift of prophecy. Attention is here called to some instances of this character in America.

The first to be noticed is that of a godly man—a well-educated and talented minister by the name of William Foy, who resided in Boston, Massachussetts. At two different times during the year 1842, the Lord came so near to him that he was wrapped in holy vision. One of these occasions was on January 18, and the other was on February 4. By invitation he went from city to city to tell of the wonderful things he had seen; and in order to accommodate the vast crowds who assembled to hear him, large halls were secured, where he related to thousands what had been shown him of the heavenly world, the loveliness of the New Jerusalem and of the angelic hosts. When dwelling upon the tender, compassionate love of Christ for poor sinners, he exhorted the unconverted to seek God, and scores responded to his tender entreaties.

Brother Foy's work continued until the year 1844, near the close of the twenty-three hundred days. Then he was favored with another manifestation of the Holy Spirit—a third vision was given—one which he did not understand. In this he was shown the pathway of the people of God through to the heavenly city. He saw a great platform, on which multitudes of people gathered. Occasionally one would drop through this platform out of sight, and of such a one it was said to him, "Apostatized." Then he saw the people rise to a second platform, and some of these also dropped through the platform out of sight; and finally a third platform appeared, which extended to the gates of the holy city. A great company gathered with those who had advanced to this platform. As he [Foy] expected the Lord Jesus to come in a very short time, he failed to recognize the fact that a third message was to follow the first and second messages of Revelation 14. Consequently the vision, to him, was inexplicable, and he ceased public speaking. After the close of the prophetic period, in the year 1845, he heard another relate the same vision, with the explanation that "the first and second messages had been given, and that a third was to follow." Soon after this, however, Brother Foy sickened and died.

Loughborough, J. N. *The Great Second Advent Movement.* Washington, D.C.: Review and Herald Pub. Assn., 1905, pp. 145-147.

Gifts of the Spirit Connected With the Message

It was not in Sweden alone that the Lord, in connection with the advent movement, spoke to His people through the gifts of His Spirit. In Scotland, in England, and also in America the Lord has instructed His people by special revelations.

William Foy's Visions

In the year 1842 there was living in Boston, Mass., a well-educated man by the name of William Foy, who was an eloquent speaker. He was a Baptist, but was preparing to take holy orders as an Episcopal minister. The Lord graciously gave him two visions in the year 1842, one on the 18th of January, the other on February 4. These visions bore clear evidence of being the genuine manifestations of the Spirit of God. He was invited from place to place to speak in the pulpits, not by the Episcopalians only, but by the Baptists and other denominations. When he spoke, he always wore the clergyman's robe, such as the ministers of that church wear in their services.

Mr. Foy's visions related to the near advent of Christ, the travels of the people of God to the heavenly city, the new earth, and the glories of the redeemed state. Having a good command of language, with fine descriptive powers, he created a sensation wherever he went. By invitation he went from city to city to tell of the wonderful things he had seen; and in order to accommodate the vast crowds who assembled to hear him, large halls were secured, where he related to thousands what had been shown him of the heavenly world, the loveliness of the New Jerusalem, and of the angelic hosts. When dwelling on the tender, compassionate love of Christ for poor sinners, he exhorted the unconverted to seek God, and scores responded to his entreaties.

Vision of the Three Steps

His work continued until the year 1844, near the close of the twenty-three hundred days. Then he was favored with another manifestation of the Holy Spirit—a third vision, one which he did not understand. In this he was shown the pathway of the people of God through to the heavenly city. He saw a great platform, or step, on which multitudes of people gathered. Occasionally one would drop through this platform out of sight, and of such a one it was said to him, "Apostatized." Then he saw the people rise to a second step, or platform, and some there also dropped through the platform out of sight. Finally a third platform appeared, which extended to the gates of the holy city. A great company gathered with those who had advanced to this platform. As he expected the Lord Jesus to come in a very short time, he failed to recognize the fact that a third message was to follow the first and second messages of Revelation 14. Consequently the vision was to him inexplainable, and he ceased public speaking. After the close of the prophetic period, in the year 1845, he heard another relate the same vision, with the explanation that "the first and second messages had been given, and that a third was to follow." Soon after this Mr. Foy sickened and died.

With such manifestations of the power of God in connection with the preaching of His coming "at the doors," and with the rejoicing of thousands who were turning from sin to serve the Lord, and to wait for His coming, the people were doubly assured that this was indeed the Lord's message to the world.

#

W i l l i a m   E l l i s   F o y

B y   R o b e r t   L .   P o t t e r

William Ellis Foy was an important figure in the Millerite movement in the 1830s and 1840s. He had several visions concerning the second coming of Christ. When this coming did not materialize, he remained a Freewill Baptist preacher. He finally came to Plantation No. 7, where he remained until his death. It is because of his prominence in the Millerite movement that this sketch of his life is provided. It should be noted at the outset that his name appears spelled as Foy and as Foye. For an introduction to the Millerite movement, see the article by Charles Francis.[1]

William E. Foy was born a free Black about 1818 somewhere near Augusta, Maine. His parents were Joseph and Elizabeth (Betsy) Foy. As a youth, he was drawn to religion. He married about 1835, and with his wife, Ann, may have had two children, one a girl named Amelia. The couple likely moved to Boston and was there in 1840-1841. It was there that Foy had his visions.[2]

When the predicted second coming of Christ did not occur in 1843, Foy stayed in the ministry and went to New Bedford, Massachusetts. His wife, Ann, must have died, because William E. Foy (age 32), a Freewill Baptist clergyman, was with his mother, Betsy (age 58), according to the 1850 U.S. Federal Census.[3] Betsy must have returned to Palermo after the Massachusetts census was taken, because she, along with her husband, Joseph (age 65), show up in the 1850 U.S. Federal Census in Palermo, Maine.[4] Almost, but not quite, an example of being in two places at once!

William E. Foy married Caroline T. Griffin of Gardiner, daughter of Reuben and Fanny Griffin, at Augusta on September 24, 1851, the ceremony being performed by Rev. J. Stevens.[5] A son, Orrin, must have been born about 1852, and a girl, Laura, soon arrived about 1856. Caroline must have died soon after. Orrin lived to 1920 and had many children.

In the 1860 U.S. Federal Census William E. Foy (age 37), a Freewill Baptist clergyman, was living in Burnham, Waldo County, Maine. There were three children, Amelia (age 23), Orrin (age 7), and Henrietta (age 4), and William E. Foy's mother, Betsy (age 73).[6]

Not long after the close of the Civil War, "Rev. William E. Fay [spell-

194

ing!], a colored evangelist, organized a 'Christian Church' of 25 members at Otter Creek, Mount Desert. A few years later, Rev. Andrew Gray came to Otter Creek and wrought a great deal of good."[7] Apparently Foy left.

Rev. William E. Foy moved to Plantation No. 7, which is just east of the town of Sullivan and north of Gouldsboro. He arrived there and began to purchase property in late 1868. Thus William E. Foy bought a plot of land from William Johnson of Plantation No. 7 on January 10, 1868, on the north side of the Public Road. The price was $10.[8] Also, William E. Foy bought a small plot of land from Isaac Bunker on the Public Road next to the Doyle place on the south side of the Public Road. The date of the purchase was November 15, 1869; however, the deed was not registered until March 26, 1894. The price was $5.[9]

In 1870 William Foy (age 54) was listed as a preacher, living with son Orrin (age 17), a mariner, both in Plantation No. 7.[10]

Probably being lonely, William Foy decided to marry again, and he either went to Portland to propose to Plancentia W. Rose (first named spelled a variety of ways) or proposed by mail. When she accepted, she came to Bangor either by rail or steamer. They were married in Bangor July 5, 1873, by H. H. Andrews, J.P.[11] Amazing for a preacher to be married by a justice of the peace!

We note that Foy's mother, Betsy, is no longer with Foy, nor is Amelia or Henrietta. Could Henrietta be Laura?

Then William E. Foy sold both parcels in Plantation No. 7 to Percentia (spelling?) on August 30, 1875.[12] This probably was to avoid having to go through probate court if W. E. Foy died before Percentia.

William E. Foy (age 65) and Percentia (age 49) were living in Plantation No. 7 in 1880 according to the 1880 U.S. Federal Census.[13] It should be noted that Foy is now spelled Foye, and the name stays the same thenceforth.

There is in the Sullivan-Sorrento Historical Society's collection a book by Edward A. Johnson, who was clerk of Plantation No. 7 from 1865 to 1884.[14] This book lists voters, scholars, assessed taxes, intentions of marriage, etc.—a typical town record and a treasure of information about a little-known area. Therefore it is remarkable that Foye is not mentioned at all, even though the Plantation record covers both 1870 and 1880, for both of which the Federal Census indicated Foye was living in Plantation No. 7. Why? Probably, Foy, a Black male, was not allowed to vote, and hence was not listed as a voter in Plantation No. 7. The Fifteenth Amendment to the Constitution, ratified February 3, 1870, provided that all citizens (males!), regardless of race, were entitled to vote. Probably it took a while for this law to get to Plantation No. 7.

It should be of some interest that in the 1881 Colby *Atlas of Hancock County,* which is cadastral in format, Foy's residence is shown on the map of Sullivan on page 44, which borders on Plantation No. 7. The Foy residence is shown on the south side of the Public Road.[15]

While residing in Plantation No. 7, Foy built a house for Percentia and himself, which is gone, and he built another where Alvah and Ila Griffin lived. This house still stands. He participated in local affairs, holding meetings in local halls, etc.[16]

Son Orrin was living with his father in 1870, but after William Foy's marriage to Percentia, he moved away, living on an island off Schoodic Point. Orrin then moved to Milbridge, where he found Bessie Roberts. Orrin remained a fisherman/laborer to the end of his days.

William E. Foy died in Plantation No. 7 on November 9, 1893, and is buried in Birch Tree Cemetery in Sullivan. The handsome stone marker also lists Laura, age 7. His name on the stone marker is given as Foye. His death certificate was reported in Steuben; apparently some administrative affairs in Plantation No. 7 were reported in Steuben. The death certificate was signed by a Sullivan physician, Fred Bridgeham, M.D. The area of Plantation No. 7 where Foy lived up to his death was annexed to Sullivan in 1895, about a year after his death.

Percentia W. Foy sold both parcels deeded to her by her husband to F. Spichtig and T. E. Call on March 15, 1894, for $80.[17] Percentia then lived with the Jesse White family on Punkinville Road in Sullivan until her death December 24, 1908. Her death notice is in the Sullivan Town Records, signed by R. H. Black, M.D. Her age in the death record was 81 years, 11 months, and 27 days. According to L. C. Johnson, she is buried alongside her husband in Birch Tree Cemetery.[18]

Orrin Foy and Bessie Roberts must have married about 1895, although no record of the marriage has turned up. Bessie must have been born about 1878. A list of their children with their approximate birth dates is given in the table, along with other information.

Children of Orrin and Bessie Foy

	Birth Date	Other Information
Lucy	1896	Had a Negro female child June 14, 1920, Steuben
Willard	1898	
Loring	1900	
Donald	1902	
Granville	1906	Died Lewiston Feb. 6, 1986
Laura	1908	
Dale	1912	
Russel	1913	
Lester	1915	
Blanch A.	1916	Died Apr. 17, 1918, Milbridge
Carl	1918	Died 1933, Bangor; buried in Evergreen Cemetery, Milbridge
George	1920	Stillborn, June 5, 1920, Harrington

Bessie died in childbirth, with George: Harrington Death Records, June 5, 1920, pp. 54, 55.

Orrin died June 10, 1920.

In the 1900 U.S. Federal Census of Gouldsboro, there is listed Winfield Foye, Black, age 15, or born about 1885.[19] The name Foye and his notation as Black make it likely that he was of the Foye family. It is also likely that his father was Orrin (writer's opinion!).

The Orrin, Bessie, and Winfield Foyes were at one time living on Dyer Island, part of Harrington. In a book by Charles McLane,[20] Orrin, Bessie, and Winfield are mentioned as living at South West Cove on Dyer Island. The 1910 U.S. Federal Census listed in the book gives Orrin (age 62) and Bessie (age 32) with eight in the family, which agrees with the list of children (six) born before 1910, plus the two parents.

While the track left by Orrin seems fairly complete, that of Winfield appears to be nearly beyond recall, probably because of an unofficial name change.

I thank Jeff Brown of the Main State Archives, Charlene Clemons of the Ellsworth Library, and C. E. Nichols of Harrington for help in obtaining information about Rev. William Ellis Foye and his family.

    —Robert L. Potter

      September 2004

---

[1] *Discover Maine:* Greater Bangor Region (1997), p. 36.

[2] 1840 U.S. Federal Census, Boston, Ward 11, Suffolk County, Massachusetts; Delbert Baker, *The Unknown Prophet* (Hagerstown, Md.: Review and Herald Pub. Assn., 1987).

[3] 1850 U.S. Federal Census, 25 July, New Bedford, Massachusetts.

[4] 1850 U.S. Federal Census, 19 September, Palermo, Maine.

[5] Elizabeth Keene Young, Benjamin Lewis Keene, *Marriage Notices From the Maine Farmer, 1833-1852* (Heritage Books, Inc, 1995), p. 143.

[6] 1860 U.S. Federal Census, Waldo County, Maine.

[7] *The Island of Mount Desert Register* (Auburn, Maine: Lawton, Jordan, and Maddox, 1909-1910), p. 52.

[8] Hancock County Registry of Deeds, received Nov. 24, 1868, vol. 133, p. 11.

[9] Hancock County Registry of Deeds, received Mar. 26, 1894, vol. 281, p. 212.

[10] 1870 U.S. Federal Census, Plantation No. 7, Hancock County, Maine.

[11] *Marriage Returns of Penobscot County Prior to 1892* (Rockland, Maine: Picton Press, 1994), p. 587.

[12] Hancock County Registry of Deeds, received Sept. 17, 1875, vol. 153, p. 120.

[13] 1880 U.S. Federal Census, Plantation No. 7, Hancock County, Maine.

[14] Sullivan-Sorento Historical Society Accession No. 85, p. 73.

[15] George N. Colby, comp., *Atlas of Hancock County, Maine* (Ellsworth, Maine: S. F. Colby and Co., 1881).

[16] Leila Clark Johnson, *Sullivan and Sorrento Since 1760* (Ellsworth, Maine: Hancock County Pub. Co., 1953), p. 36.

[17] Hancock County Registry of Deeds, Mar. 15, 1894, received Mar. 26, 1894, vol. 281, p. 214.

[18] Johnson, pp. 65, 66.

[19] 1900 U.S. Federal Census, Gouldsboro, Hancock County, Maine.

[20] Charles B. McLane, *Islands of the Mid-Maine Coast: Mount Desert to Machias* (Falmouth, Maine: Kennebec River Press, 1989), Vol. II, pp. 190, 191, 338.

A Chronology of the
Life of William Foy

1818	Born William Ellis Foy to Joseph and Elizabeth Foy in Kennebec County, Maine.
1833	The Foys reside in Palermo, Maine.
1835	William Foy converted and baptized by Silas Curtis in Augusta, Maine.
c. 1836	Foy weds Ann (maiden name unknown).
c. 1837	The Foys have a daughter, Amelia.
c. 1840	The Foys move to Boston, Massachusetts.
Jan. 18, 1842	Foy has his first vision in a religious gathering at venue on Southock (also Southark, Southack, currently Phillips) Street in Boston.
Jan. 19-Feb. 3, 1842	Foy prints first vision.
Feb. 4-5, 1842	Foy has second vision in religious gathering on May Street in Boston.
Feb. 6, 1842	Pastor J. B. Husted and several members of Second Methodist Episcopal Church request Foy to share his visions the next day at their church. Foy consents.
Feb. 7, 1842	Foy speaks on his visions to Second Methodist Episcopal Church on Bromfield Street in Boston.
March-May 1842	Foy commences a speaking tour on his visions. The Harmon family (including daughter Ellen) attend Foy's lectures and hear about his visions.
June-August 1842	Foy ends tour and practices a trade, temporarily suspending speaking engagements. During this time the Foys move to Portland, Maine.
1843	Renowned artist William Matthew Prior paints portraits of Foy's cousin, Nancy Lawson, and her husband, William Lawson.
Feb. 10, 1844	The Portland *Tribune* runs racially derogatory piece titled "When Will Wonders Cease?" mocking the Millerites for inviting a Black

	man who had "dreams and prognostications" to Portland to speak to them.
Feb. 27, 1844	Foy cancels a speaking appointment at the Casco Street church in Portland, Maine.
c. Summer 1844	Foy has third and fourth visions.
Oct. 23, 1844	Foy is disappointed along with other Millerites when Jesus does not return.
Jan. 3, 1845	Foy registers *The Christian Experience of William E. Foy* with the clerk's office of the district court of the state of Maine, and it is entered according to an act of Congress. *The Christian Experience of William E. Foy* is published.
1845	William Foy attends meeting in which Ellen White describes her vision. Foy interrupts White, exclaiming that he had had a similar revelation. Afterward the two have a discussion.
c. pre-1850	Ann Foy dies. Joseph Foy, William's father, dies. Foy's mother, Elizabeth, moves in with Foy. Foy accepts call to pastor racially mixed congregation in New Bedford, Massachusetts.
Sept. 24, 1851	Foy marries Caroline T. Griffin.
1852	A son, Orrin, is born.
1855	Foy pastors the Freewill Baptist church in Chelsea, Maine.
1856	A daughter, Lauraitta (sometimes Laura or Henrietta), is born.
1856-1860	Caroline Foy dies.
1860	William and his mother, Elizabeth, along with 23-year-old Amelia, appear in 1860 census for Brunswick, Maine. William, Amelia, Orrin, and Lauraitta move to Burnham, Maine, and live with a family called the Whittens.
1863	Lauraitta Foy dies. Foy moves to southern Maine.
c. 1865	Foy organizes a "Christian Church" of 25 members in Mount Desert Island, Maine.
Jan. 10, 1868	Foy purchases land from a William Johnson in Plantation No. 7, Maine (Hancock County),

	just east of Sullivan and north of Gouldsboro.
Nov. 15, 1869	Foy purchases small plot of land from Isaac Bunker in Plantation No. 7 for $5. Deed is registered on March 26, 1894.
1870	Elizabeth Foy dies.
	Foy is listed in Plantation No. 7 census as 54 years of age, a preacher, living with 17-year-old son Orrin, a mariner.
July 5, 1873	William Foy weds Parcentia W. Rose.
Aug. 30, 1875	Foy sells Plantation No. 7 real estate to Parcentia.
1880	William and Parcentia Foy are listed in census for Township No. 7, Maine. William is identified as a preacher. William begins spelling name "Foye."
1892	John N. Loughborough's *Rise and Progress of the Seventh-day Adventists* is published, discussing Foy on pages 70, 71.
Jan. 31, 1893	Loughborough speaks of Foy at length at the General Conference session, held in Battle Creek, Michigan.
Nov. 9, 1893	William Foy dies in Plantation No. 7, Maine. He is buried in Birch Tree Cemetery in East Sullivan, Maine.

Bibliography
Original Sources

Periodicals

Loughborough, J. N. "Early Experiences." *General Conference Daily Bulletin,* Mar. 18, 1891, pp. 113, 114.

————. "The Prophetic Gift." *Review and Herald,* July 18, 1899, p. 2.

————. "The Study of the Testimonies—No. 4." *General Conference Daily Bulletin,* Jan. 31, Feb. 1, 1893, p. 59.

Books

Colby, George N., comp. *Atlas of Hancock County, Maine.* Ellsworth, Maine: S. F. Colby and Co., 1881.

Homans, Isaac Smith. *Sketches of Boston, Past and Present.* Boston: Phillips, Sampson, and Co., 1851, p. 85.

Johnson, Leila Clark. *Sullivan and Sorrento Since 1760.* Ellsworth, Maine: Hancock County Pub. Co., 1953, pp. 65, 66.

Kingsbury, Henry D., and Simeon L. Deyo. *Illustrated History of Kennebec County, Maine, 1625, 1792, 1892.* New York: H. W. Blake & Co., 1892, part 2, p. 1042.

Loughborough, J. N. *Rise and Progress of the Seventh-day Adventists.* Battle Creek, Mich.: General Conference of Seventh-day Adventists, 1892, pp 70, 71.

————. *The Great Second Advent Movement.* Washington, D.C.: Review and Herald Pub. Assn., 1905, pp. 145-147.

White, Ellen G. *Manuscript Releases.* Silver Spring, Md.: Ellen G. White Estate, 1993, vol. 17, pp. 95-97.

Williamson, Joseph. *A Bibliography of the State of Maine From the Earliest Period to 1891.* Portland, Maine: Thurston Print, 1896, vol. 1, p. 448.

Census Records

1840 U.S. Federal Census, Boston, Ward 11, Suffolk County, Massachusetts. (Foy, William).

1841 U.S. Boston [Massachusetts] Directory, p. 483.

1850 U.S. Federal Census, New Bedford, Massachusetts, July 25 (Foy, William).

1850 U.S. Federal Census, Palermo, Maine, September 19 (Foy, William).

1850 U.S. Census, State of Massachusetts, Bristol County (Foy, William).

1860 U.S. Federal Census, Waldo County, Maine (Foy, William).

1860 U.S. Census, State of Maine, Cumberland County (Foy, William).

1870 U.S. Federal Census, Plantation No. 7, Hancock County, Maine (Foy, William).

1880 U.S. Federal Census, Plantation No. 7, Hancock County, Maine (Foye, William).

1900 U.S. Federal Census, Gouldsboro, Hancock County, Maine (Foye, Winfield).

Hancock County [Maine] Registry of Deeds, 1868. Received November 24. Vol. 133, p. 11.

Hancock County [Maine] Registry of Deeds, 1875. Received September 17. Vol. 133, p. 120.

Hancock County [Maine] Registry of Deeds, 1894. Received March 26. Vol. 133, p. 214.

Hancock County [Maine] Registry of Deeds, 1894. Received March 26. Vol. 133, p. 212.

Marriage Returns of Penobscot County Prior to 1892. Rockland, Maine: Picton Press, 1994, p. 587.

The Island of Mount Desert Register. Auburn, Maine: Lawton-Jordan Co., 1910, p. 52.

Newspapers

Foy, William Ellis. "Notice." Portland *Advertiser*, Feb. 27, 1844.

"When Will Wonders Cease?" Portland *Tribune*, Feb. 10, 1844, p. 351.

Pamphlets

Foy, William E. *The Christian Experience of William E. Foy Together With the Two Visions He Received in the Months of January and February 1842.* Portland, Maine: J. and C. H. Pearson, 1845.

Unpublished Manuscripts

Foy, William E. "Egypt's Land." Center for Adventist Research at Andrews University.

White, Ellen G. "Interview With Mrs. E. G. White Regarding Early Experiences." Manuscript 131, 1906. In Ellen G. White. *Manuscript Releases.* Silver Spring, Md.: Ellen G. White Estate, 1993, vol. 17, pp. 95-97.

Secondary Sources

Articles

Allen, Gregory. "William Foy: God's Bold Messenger." *Youth Ministry Accent*, April-June 2000, pp. 10-12.

Baker, Benjamin. "The Career of *The Unknown Prophet*." *Adventist Today*, May-June 2012, pp. 14, 15.

Baker, Delbert W. "In Search of Roots, Part One." *Adventist Review*, Feb. 4, 1993, pp. 12, 14.

———. "Questions and Answers About the Unknown Prophet, William Foy." *Spectrum*, May 1987, pp. 24, 25.

———. "William Foy: Messenger to the Advent Believers." *Adventist Review*, Jan. 14, 1988, pp. 8-10.

———, and Ronald D. Graybill. "William Ellis Foy: A Black Adventist Prophet Rediscovered." *Columbia Union Visitor*, Feb. 15, 1985, pp. 4-6.

Burns, Gary. "William Foy: A Message for Today." *Lake Union Herald*, February 2005, p. 11.

Burt, Merlin D. "Center for Adventist Research Replicates Foy Tract." *Lake Union Herald*, February 2005, p. 36.

Carscallen, Leona. "Except as We Forget." *The Youth's Instructor*, Oct. 6, 1959, p. 20.

Crandall, Walter T. "The Spirit of Prophecy." *The Youth's Instructor*, Jan. 27, 1970, p. 5.

Edison, Richard G. "William Foy: I Will Go." *Youth Ministry Accent*, April-June 2000, pp. 34, 35.

"First of Three." *Adventist Review*, Jan. 19, 2012, p. 7.

Graybill, Ronald D., and Delbert W. Baker. "William Ellis Foy: A Black Prophet Rediscovered." *Columbia Union Visitor*, Feb. 15, 1985, pp. 4-6.

Hale, D. U. "New England Conference Report." *Atlantic Union Gleaner*, Feb. 6, 1924, p. 11.

Hoyt, Frederick. "We Lift Up Our Voices Like a Trumpet: Millerites in Portland, Maine." *Spectrum*, May 1987, pp. 19, 20.

Hulse, V. P. "To keep Thee in the Way." *Columbia Union Visitor*, July 8, 1926, p. 2.

Nix, James R. "The Third Prophet Spoke Forth." *Adventist Review*, Dec. 4, 1986, p. 22.

Peterson, A. W. "Where There Is No Vision the People Perish." *The Youth's Instructor*, Oct. 17, 1944.

Poirier, Tim. "Black Forerunner to Ellen White: William E. Foy." *Spectrum*, August 1987, pp. 23-28.

Simmons, Kate. "Pioneering Heroes of Black Adventism." *Outlook*, February 2006, pp. 10, 11.

Singleton, H. D. "North American Regional Department." *Adventist Review*, June 22, 1966, p. 13.

Spicer, W. A. "The Exodus and the Advent Movement." *Columbia Union Visitor*, May 17, 1911, p. 3.

Strayer, Brian E. "A Colorful Patchwork Quilt." *Adventist Heritage*, Summer 1998, p. 25.

Vandeman, George E. "The Writings of Ellen G. White." *The Youth's Instructor*, Apr. 5, 1955, p. 25.

Books

Andross, Matilda Erickson. *Story of the Advent Message*. Washington, D.C.: Review and Herald Pub. Assn., 1926. P. 58.

Baker, Benjamin J. *Crucial Moments*. Hagerstown, Md.: Review and Herald Pub. Assn., 2005, pp. 15-26.

————, et al., eds. *People of Providence*. Huntsville, Ala.: Oakwood University Press, 2010, p. 56.

Baker, Delbert W. *The Unknown Prophet*. Hagerstown, Md.: Review and Herald Pub. Assn., 1987.

————, ed. *Telling the Story*. Loma Linda, Calif.: Loma Linda University, 1996.

————, and Susan Baker, eds. *Lives With Impact*. Huntsville, Ala.: Oakwood University Press, 2009, pp. 418-420.

Birch, Canute. *A Third Great Disappointment for the Remnant?* Ringgold, Ga.: TEACH Services, 2012, pp. 30-32.

Bull, Malcolm, and Keith Lockhart. *Seeking a Sanctuary: Seventh-day Adventism and the American Dream*. Indianapolis: Indiana University Press, 2006, p. 440.

Bunch, Taylor G. *Exodus and Advent Movements in Type and Antitype*. Washington, D.C.: Review and Herald Pub. Assn., 1937, p. 52.

Burt, Merlin D. *Adventist Pioneer Places: New York and New England*. Hagerstown, Md.: Review and Herald Pub. Assn., 2011, pp. 2-5, 42, 53, 54, 72.

————, ed. *Christian Experience*. Berrien Springs, Mich.: Andrews University Press, 2005.

Clark, Jerome L. *1844: Religious Movements*. Nashville: Southern Pub. Assn., 1968, Vol. I, pp. 72, 73.

Collins, Norma J. *Heartwarming Stories of Adventist Pioneers*. Hagerstown, Md.: Review and Herald Pub. Assn., 2005, book 1, pp. 92-95.

Coon, Roger W. *A Gift of Light*. Hagerstown, Md.: Review and Herald Pub. Assn., 1983, pp. 16, 26, 27.

————. *The Great Visions of Ellen G. White*. Hagerstown, Md.: Review and Herald Pub. Assn., 1992, pp. 33, 34, 38, 151.

Douglass, Herbert E. *Messenger of the Lord*. Nampa, Idaho: Pacific Press Pub. Assn., 1998, pp. 39, 135, 576.

Dudley, Charles E. *The Genealogy of Ellen Gould Harmon White.*
Collegedale, Tenn.: The College Press, 1999, p. 28.

———. *Thou Who Hast Brought Us . . .* Brushton, N.Y.: TEACH Services,
1997, pp. 58, 77.

———. *Thou Who Hast Brought Us Thus Far on Our Way.* Nashville: Dudley
Publications, 2000, pp. xxi, 49, 70, 71.

Ellen G. White Encyclopedia (forthcoming). Ed. Denis Fortin and Jerry Moon.
Hagerstown, Md.: Review and Herald Pub. Assn., s.v. "Foy, William Ellis."

General Conference of SDA Department of Education. *The Story of Our
Church.* Mountain View, Calif.: Pacific Press Pub. Assn., 1956, p. 188.

General Conference of SDA Youth Department. *Church Heritage Manual.*
Silver Spring, Md.: General Conference of Seventh-day Adventists,
2002, p. 25.

Graham, Roy E. *Ellen G. White: Cofounder of the Seventh-day Adventist Church.*
New York: Peter Lang, 1985. Pp. 53, 67.

Hodges, Clarence E. *This Far by Faith.* Hagerstown, Md.: Review and Herald
Pub. Assn., 1998, pp. 21, 22.

Horton, James Oliver, and Lois E. Horton. *Black Bostonians.* New York:
Homes and Meier, 2000.

Hoyt, Frederick. "Ellen White's Hometown: Portland, Maine, 1827-1846." In
Gary Land, ed. *The World of Ellen G. White.* Hagerstown, Md.: Review
and Herald Pub. Assn., 1987, pp. 13-32.

Hurt, James E. *First National Assembly of Black Churches.* Evansville, Ind.:
Bertram Books, 1984, p. 156.

Jemison, T. Housel. *A Prophet Among You.* Mountain View, Calif.: Pacific
Press Pub. Assn., 1955, pp. 485-489.

Jones, Clifford R. *James K. Humphrey and the Sabbath-day Adventists.*
Jackson, Miss.: University Press of Mississippi, 2006, p. 86.

Justiss, Jacob. *Angels in Ebony.* Toledo, Ohio: Jet Printing Service, 1975,
pp. 14-17.

Knight, George R. *Lest We Forget.* Hagerstown, Md.: Review and Herald Pub.
    Assn., 2008, p. 28.

————. *Millennial Fever and the End of the World.* Nampa, Idaho: Pacific
    Press Pub. Assn., 1993, pp. 118, 119, 355.

————. *William Miller and the Rise of Adventism.* Nampa, Idaho: Pacific Press
    Pub. Assn., 2010, pp. 99, 100.

Land, Gary. *The A to Z of the Seventh-day Adventists.* Lanham, Md.: The Scare-
    crow Press, 2009, pp. 104, 105.

————. *Dictionary of Seventh-day Adventists.* Lanham, Md.: The Scarecrow
    Press, 2005, pp. 104, 105.

Loughborough, John N. *Heavenly Visions.* Comp. Leon Schmitke. Mentone,
    Calif.: Leon Schmitke, 1984, p. 27.

Makapela, Alven. *The Problem With Africanity in the Seventh-day Adventist
    Church.* Lewiston, N.Y.: Edwin Mellon Press, 1996.

Marshall, Norwida, and Steven Norman III, eds. *A Star Gives Light:
    Seventh-day Adventist African American Heritage.* Decatur, Ga.:
    Southern Union Conference of Seventh-day Adventists, 1989, p. 13.

Maxwell, C. Mervyn. *Tell It to the World: The Story of Seventh-day Adventists.*
    Mountain View, Calif.: Pacific Press Pub. Assn., 1976, pp. 44, 45.

Meister, Charles W. *Year of the Lord.* Jefferson, N.C.: McFarland & Co., 1983,
    pp. 18, 19.

Morgan, Douglas. *Lewis C. Sheafe: Apostle to Black America.* Hagerstown,
    Md.: Review and Herald Pub. Assn., 2010, pp. 117, 124.

Nix, James R., comp. *Memorable Dates From Our Adventist Past.* Silver
    Spring, Md.: North American Division Office of Education, 1989, pp.
    13, 14.

Numbers, Ronald L. *Prophetess of Health.* New York: William B. Eerdmans,
    2008, pp. 60, 61.

Painter, Nell Irvin. *Sojourner Truth: A Life, A Symbol.* New York: W. W. Nor-
    ton and Co., 1997, p. 81.

Pinn, Anthony B., ed. *African American Religious Cultures.* Santa Barbara, Calif.: Greenwood Press, 2009, pp. 363, 364.

Price, H. H., and Gerald E. Talbot. *Maine's Visible Black History: The First Chronicle of Its People.* Gardiner, Maine: Tilbury House Publishers, 2006, p. 385.

Reynolds, Louis B. *We Have Tomorrow.* Hagerstown, Md.: Review and Herald Pub. Assn., 1984, pp. 19-21.

Robbins, Larry, comp. *Lest We Forget.* South Lancaster, Mass.: Atlantic Union Conference, vol. 1, pp. 5, 8, 67.

————, comp. *Lest We Forget.* South Lancaster, Mass.: Atlantic Union Conference, vol. 4, pp. 4, 23.

Rock, Calvin B. *Go On! Vital Messages for Today's Christian.* Hagerstown, Md.: Review and Herald Pub. Assn., 1994, p. 100.

Schwarz, Richard W., and Floyd Greenleaf. *Light Bearers.* Nampa, Idaho: Pacific Press Pub. Assn., 2000, p. 62.

Taves, Ann. *Fits, Trances, and Visions: Experiencing Religion and Explaining Experience From Wesley to James.* Princeton, N.J.: Princeton University Press, 1999, pp. 158, 159.

The Seventh-day Adventist Encyclopedia. Hagerstown, Md.: Review and Herald Pub. Assn., 1996, s.v. "Foy, William E."

Vance, Laura L. *Seventh-day Adventism in Crisis: Gender and Sectarian Change in an Emerging Religion.* Champaign, Ill.: University of Illinois Press, 1999, pp. 37, 258.

Veith, Walter J. *Truth Matters: Escaping the Labyrinth of Error.* Roseville, Calif.: Amazing Discoveries, 2002, p. 410.

White, Arthur L. *Ellen G. White—Messenger to the Remnant.* Washington, D.C.: Review and Herald Pub. Assn., 1969, pp. 29-39.

Dissertations

Baker, Benjamin J. "'I Do Not Mean to Live or Die a Coward': An Examination of Ellen G. White's Lifelong Relationship to Black

People." Ph.D. Diss., Howard University, 2001, pp. 15-21, 41-57.

Baker, Delbert W. "The Dynamics of Communication and African-American Progress in the Seventh-day Adventist Organization: A Historical Descriptive Analysis." Ph.D. Diss., Howard University, 1993.

Papers

Allen, Gregory John. "William E. Foy: An Apologetic." Term paper, Seventh-day Adventist Theological Seminary, Andrews University, 1979.

Amos, Curtis. "An Examination of the Visions of William E. Foy." Term paper, Seventh-day Adventist Theological Seminary, Andrews University, 1978.

Baker, Delbert W. "William E. Foy: Part of God's Design." Term paper, Seventh-day Adventist Theological Seminary, Andrews University, 1977.

Taliaferro, William Maurice. "The First Two Visions of William Foy and Their Affinity With Prophetic Sources." Term paper, Seventh-day Adventist Theological Seminary, Andrews University, 1979.

Unpublished Manuscripts

Potter, Robert L. "William Ellis Foy." Center for Adventist Research, Andrews University, 2004.

Ellen G. White Estate/Center for Adventist Research Documents

Burt, Merlin, and James R. Nix. "William E. Foy Research Materials." Center for Adventist Research, Andrews University, 2009.

Poirier, Tim. "Comments Regarding Literary Parallels Between William Foy and Ellen White." Silver Spring, Md.: Ellen G. White Estate, 1985. Document File 231.

————. "The Visions of William Foy and Hazen Foss: An Examination of the Historical Sources." Silver Spring, Md.: Ellen G. White Estate, 1983. Document File 231.

White, Arthur L. "Arthur L. White on William Ellis Foy." Silver Spring, Md.: Ellen G. White Estate. Document File 231.

A Guide to Seventh-day Adventist History Resources on the Internet

Web Site Address: www.adventistarchives.org/DocArchives.asp

Operator: General Conference Office of Archives, Statistics, and Research

Description: This site boasts approximately 2 million pages of free, downloadable materials on Adventist history. Available are every major Adventist periodical, yearbook, annual statistical report, and Sabbath school quarterly; hundreds of images, maps, and charts; statistics and research papers; as well as an impressive selection of complete books. The documents are arranged in a logical and intuitive way, and are available in PDF format. GC Archives also has a Twitter page (twitter.com/GCArchives), Facebook page (www.facebook.com/GC.SDA.Archives?ref=ts&fref=ts), and YouTube channel (www.youtube.com/user/SDAArchives) with more than 300 videos on church history.

Web Site Address: www.whiteestate.org/

Operator: Ellen G. White Estate, Inc.

Description: The White Estate has done much to keep up with current trends by making the writings of church cofounder Ellen G. White available to modern browsers. Besides the above Web site, which features answers to frequently asked questions; brief and useful introductions to Ellen White, Adventist pioneers, and their world; a kids' section; a television program; more than 2,000 photographs; and an app, the White Estate recently debuted an additional Web site with White's writings available in multiple languages (https://egwwritings.org/). Everything previously only available on the expensive CD ROM is now free.

Web Site Address: www.andrews.edu/library/car/index.html

Operator: Center for Adventist Research (CAR) at Andrews University

Description: CAR possesses a number of features that will have those interested in Adventist history coming back again and again. Immediately useful is the Seventh-day Adventist periodical index (www.andrews.edu/library/car/sdapiindex.html), in which searches for articles in Adventist periodicals can be performed. Most of the tens of thousands of articles in this database can be read and downloaded on the previously mentioned adventistarchives.org. A sister site is the Seventh-day Adventist obituary index (www.andrews.edu/library/car/sdapiobits.html), in which one can quickly find out the life dates of individuals and read their obituaries. CAR also contains an extensive photo collection (www.andrews.edu/library/car/photosearch.html) and library catalog (www.andrews.edu/library/index.cgi) and links to other helpful sites.

Web Site Address: http://blacksdahistory.org/

  Operator: Center for Ethnic Adventist History Studies

  Description: This site specializes in information and materials on Black Seventh-day Adventism, boasting more than 350 Web pages containing resources, downloadable documents and books, videos, time lines, statistics, rare photographs, and an extensive obituary section. Also of note are monthly features such as Quote of the Month, Book of the Month, Video of the Month, and Essay of the Month. Be sure to check out the companion YouTube channel (www.youtube.com/user/Blacksdahistory).

Web Site Address: http://archives.llu.edu/cdm/

  Operator: Loma Linda University (LLU)

  Description: The LLU digital archive offers an invaluable service to those wishing to access the Adventist past, including every issue of the only periodical solely on Adventist history, *Adventist Heritage* (http://archives.llu.edu/cdm/landingpage/collection/advhert). *Adventist Heritage* was distinguished for its intriguing articles and unique layout, and its pages will still intrigue contemporary readers. The digital archive additionally features hundreds of photographs and interesting artifacts from yesteryear.

Web Site Address: http://library.puc.edu/adventist/sda_resources.shtml

  Operator: Nelson Memorial Library, Pacific Union College

  Description: This Web page primarily directs to other sites, although Gary Shearer's suite of bibliographies are extremely helpful to those searching for books, articles, and dissertations in a particular area of Adventist history and general history (http://library.puc.edu/heritage/bib-index.shtml).

Web Site Address: www.adventistheritage.org/

    Operator: Adventist Heritage Ministry

    Description: The strength of this Web site is the photographs of original Adventist buildings and locales. Visits and tours to these historic spots, as well as to the Historic Adventist Village in Battle Creek, Michigan, can be scheduled here. Also at this address is a well-equipped store with resources on SDA history.

Web Site Address: /www.adventistreview.org/

    Operator: *Adventist Review*

    Description: This daily-updated Web site of the general paper of the Seventh-day Adventist Church not only has scores of searchable articles on Adventist history, but a magazine archive (www.adventistreview.org/article/3/archives).

Web Site Address: www.adventisthistory.org.uk/documents.php

    Operator: Newbold College

    Description: The British Union Conference historical archive is a rich resource on Adventism in the United Kingdom and Ireland, replete with photographs, documents, and useful links.

Web Site Address: www.aplib.org/

    Operator: Adventist Pioneer Library

    Description: The strength of this Web site is its short but informative videos (www.aplib.org/?page_id=618) and concise written biographies (www.aplib.org/?page_id=12) on Millerite and Adventist pioneers.

Web Site Address: http://news.adventist.org/

    Operator: Seventh-day Adventist Church Adventist News Network (ANN)

    Description: Although this site is concerned with breaking news, of course old news is history. Here you will find archives of news broadcasts, photos, and stories, all very handy in understanding the Adventist Church. There are also frequent spotlights on the SDA past, including the weekly "This Week in Adventist History" segment on the ANN video.

INDEX

ADVENTIST PIONEER

JOSEPH BATES
The Real Founder of Seventh-day Adventism
George Knight
Hardcover. 978-0-8280-1815-4

E. J. WAGGONER
From the Physician of Good News to Agent of Division
Woodrow W. Whidden II
Hardcover. 978-0-8280-1982-8

LEWIS C. SHEAFE
Apostle to Black America
Douglas Morgan
Hardcover. 978-0-8280-2397-9

Lest We Forget ...

"We have nothing to fear for the future, except as we shall forget the way the Lord has led us, and His teaching in our past history." —ELLEN G. WHITE.

JAMES WHITE
Innovator and Overcome
Gerald Wheeler
Hardcover. 978-0-8280-17

SERIES

These biographical sketches of early Adventist pioneers emphasize the valuable contributions each one made to the Seventh-day Adventist Church.

JOHN HARVEY KELLOGG
Pioneering Health Reformer

Richard W. Schwarz
Hardcover. 978-0-8280-1939-2

W. W. PRESCOTT
Forgotten Giant of Adventism's Second Generation

Gilbert M. Valentine
Hardcover. 978-0-8280-1892-0

A. T. JONES
Point Man on Adventism's Charismatic Frontier

George Knight
Hardcover. 978-0-8280-2562-1

J. N. LOUGHBOROUGH
The Last of the Adventist Pioneers

Brian E. Strayer
Hardcover. 978-0-8280-2662-8

Take the Tour

Visit the sites where the Adventist faith began: the pioneers' homes and churches, the sites of births and deaths, the special places where visions descended and revival arose.

Adventist Pioneer Places includes:

- maps
- current, color photographs of landmarks
- historic photographs
- stories that illuminate the lives of the pioneers
- GPS coordinates

Merlin D. Burt's handbook serves as an invaluable guide for a trip in the family car or for a virtual tour taken in the comfort of your favorite reading chair.

You will feel inspired as you walk in the footsteps of people who, though weak and fallible, were used by God in remarkable ways to establish a global community of believers and begin a series of events that would eventually touch your own life.

Hardcover. 978-0-8280-2568-3

Review&Herald

An exciting way for kids to learn church history!

AUDIO CD 22 CDs, 978-0-8280-2063-3 **MP3** 2 MP3 CDs, 978-0-8280-2062-6 **COMPLETE SCRIPTS CD-ROM** 978-0-8280-2064-0	The creative team of Your Story Hour brings to life 115 historical stories about the development and growth of the Seventh-day Adventist church. This series begins with God's call to William Miller, concludes with the death of Ellen G. White, and tells of the wonderful and difficult years in between. Sure to be enjoyed by all ages, this collection will inspire, delight, and educate. Great to listen to in the car! Approximate total running time: 23 hours 25 minutes.